BROKEN

Before I Found Purpose

Copyright © 2020 by Anitra Woods

Printed in the United States of America

ISBN-13: 978-0-578-70545-3

Arranged by: Tammy Johnson

Edited by: SD Horton Enterprises

CONTENTS

BIO

Anitra Woods is a single mother of 3 boys and a foster mother to several others. She is also the mother of a young author. She is the founder of Big Dreamers Youth Foundation, a mentor, coach, advocate for bullied students, YPD youth director, community scientist, board secretary, and community leader for B.I.S.C.O.

Anitra enjoys working with the youth. She has been volunteering in the schools and community for over 18 years working on building youths' confidence in themselves and education.

Anitra was recognized with a community award for working with the youths in 2017, and is a two-time nominee for the Unsung Hero award.

ACKNOWLEDGEMENTS

First and foremost, I would like to give praises and thanks to God for giving me this opportunity. Had it not been for God, I wouldn't be here right now because He is the One who's given me the strength and courage to press on both mentally and spiritually, especially in times of discouragements.

My mom Joyce Adams for her understanding.

My kids Rodney Woods Jr., Dorian Woods, Ke'Shawn Woods, and Montrell Bell. Because of you, I am a better person for myself and you.

My brothers Roger and Wendell Davis. You two are #1 reason I started this journey.

To my cousin Shedrick Wilson for encouraging me in school.

My forever friend Rodney Woods Sr. Thank you for stepping up when you did.

To everyone else who may have shared some positive words with me. Thank you!

DEDICATION

To God Be The Glory

In grateful and blessed memory of

My grandpa

Joseph Adams (1919-1991)

And Godmother/Aunt

Thelma Wilson (1950-1996)

MAY THEIR MEMORY BE ETERNAL

FOREWORD

Nobody knows the trouble I've seen
Nobody knows my sorrow
Nobody knows the trouble I've seen
Glory, Hallelujah

Excerpt from African-American Spiritual

A young woman with a warm smile, in constant motion-- completing another task, continuously providing support to someone in need; this is Anitra, confident, purpose-filled, driven, and once ---**broken.**

There is an idiom that says, 'you can't judge a book by its cover.' This is true of Anitra; the calm exterior that exudes today comes from beginnings of turmoil and pain. My first encounter with Anitra was in preparation for a summer camp for community children. She was like a modern-day Pied Piper, stopping at homes as she walked to the church hall calling children in her neighborhood to come and participate, assuring mamas she would deliver the children safely back to their homes. It is during this time that I witnessed her uncanny ability to comfort a frustrated three-year-old, who could not glue his project as she also supported an overwhelmed teenager. How could a person provide the exact level of support needed by each child, and do so with compassion?

Anitra's story reveals the source of her demeanor; it is not by accident but comes from years of tears, frustration, fear, turmoil, and hurt. **Broken** provides a first-hand account of a person whose childhood naivety and the essence of young womanhood marred by a series of events that some could only imagine. **Broken** provides a vivid picture of the chains of betrayals, abuse, and disappointments as a young girl and later young woman struggle to make sense of her world.

So what about that warm smile? It comes from acknowledging the pain, releasing it, and building a new landscape of life; like the beautiful wildflowers that blanket the hills of southern California after the fires. Up from the ashes, no longer **broken**, Anitra is rising and sharing her story with others who may feel there is no hope. Her story is a seed to others, like her, to rise from the ashes.

Christine C. Hypolite, PhD
Professor of Education
Thibodaux, Louisiana

CHAPTER 1

1

PRESERVED

Back when I was around 9 or 10 years old, I remember playing in my home and having good times with my family. Everyone had smiles on their faces. I watched family and family friends come over to eat and enjoy each other's company. I especially love the holidays. Christmas is my favorite holiday; and although we might not have had much, it was just something about Christmas that always puts a smile on my face. Mom would put up this 2-foot tree that she had since she was a little girl. She said she kept it because it reminded her of her mom. Her mom passed when she was 17. She later became pregnant with me at 18. The few things she had left from her mom she kept because she was the youngest of her family and all her other siblings had everything else of her mom.

I guess you can say I was a little selfish because I hated that little tree, but I didn't understand how much it meant to her. How can you put presents under a 2-foot tree? Somehow, she did, or they covered the tree. I enjoyed Christmas and all the stories, especially the movies. My all-time favorite was *A Christmas Story*. Every night before bed, we would drink hot cocoa and make cookies. On Christmas Eve, we get to open 1 gift before bed. Christmas morning, we would be ready like any other to open our gifts. It wasn't much, but we were happy.

My next favorite holiday was *Mardi Gras*. All my family would come over. They would barbecue, making hamburgers and hot dogs for all the kids. We would be excited when we hear the police sirens and we would run outside to wait on the parade. Once the parade was over, the family didn't leave. We had fun... lots of fun. The kids would be riding around and playing, and the adults would sit around until it was time to go to the evening parade. The street would be packed with folks from all over. We lived on one of the most popular streets in our neighborhood. One of the two black parades we have in our area would roll in front our house on *Mardi Gras* day. This was a time when the older folks would look out for everyone. People would just hang out and chill, everyone smiling and having a good time.

Later, whenever you see the streets thinning out, you already knew what time it was. We all would walk down the canal and wait on the big parade. It was *Fat Tuesday*, our biggest parade ever. After the parade was over, we would just hang around on the streets, and then figure out how we were going to get all those bags of beads back home.

When we get back home, we would still be having a good time. Traffic would be so backed up, people would be hanging out of cars; and once it got dark, the 5.0s would be lit up, and it'll be like a parade of cars until like 2 a.m. in the morning. It was some of the best times I ever had. I was just a happy and content little girl. But there were days where I had the best day and the worst day of my life within hours apart.

YOUNG AND NAIVE

It all changed for me. I had no clue to what was going on because no one educated me on any of this. So, when things happen, you assume everything is ok. I remember being in elementary school when it first started happening. I was always told that my smile was pretty. After a while, I didn't smile so much. When I did, I faked it so that no one could see what I was feeling inside.

Like any other day, a family friend would hold me on his lap and rock me. I'm a kid, so I guess it was no big deal because there were always people around. He would just rock me on his lap and rub on my legs. No one ever told him anything all the years he had been doing it. It just kept happening...the same guy every time he would come over. He would say, *'hey pretty girl, come sit on my lap.'*

He would pull me by my hands so I could go to him. I would find myself in between his legs while he would grind on me. As a kid at that age, I didn't know what he was doing. He just liked to rock and tickle me. I never paid any attention if anyone was around whenever he would move me between his legs. While sitting on his lap, he would just tell me stories and rock me on his lap. This was something he'd been doing for years for as long as I knew him; and he would tell funny stories that made me laugh and continue to tickle me. Was he doing this while I was much younger? Feeling on me that way, it kills me because I can't remember.

No one told me about these things so I didn't know what was going on and what was happening to me at the time. I guess the young me thought what he was doing was acceptable. Thing is, he never said to me, *'don't tell my mom or dad.'* He would just treat me nice and buy me things. He eventually moved away and I never saw him again; only heard stories about him.

There was always another friend who would come along, and what do you know?! He did the same thing; just wasn't as much as the first guy. Knowing what I know today, I think he wasn't crazy. He was being careful not to get caught. He also knew when my mom would be home or not because he would never hold me around her.

While my mother would be gone out running errands, I'm left alone with my brothers, my dad, and his friends. As a kid, we weren't educated on drugs, sex, alcohol, or anything of that nature happening. If you're not educated, you don't know what's really going on. You don't know what's okay or what's not okay. So again, whatever was being done, you see it in your face; and you know it's happening. You just assume it is acceptable. This was a regular thing happening to me, and it was only the beginning.

CHAPTER 2

2

UNDERSTANDING THE LOSS OF A LOVED ONE

My grandfather's passing was the first time that I experienced a loss. I didn't know what I was feeling or even how to handle it. I just knew I felt this hurt. I cried and cried. I never seen so many people come together to sit down and have a conversation when someone passed. Just hearing love ones saying it's going to be okay. It wasn't so plain to me what someone dying really meant. My grandfather had a stroke a few years back, and for as long as I've known him, he was always in a wheelchair. My grandfather was my mom's dad and he lived with us in our small home, along with my two younger brothers, my mom, and dad. It was just a four-room house, so my grandfather, one of my little brothers, and I shared the living room. We had a big queen size bed that we slept in every night.

Every morning around 4 a.m. or 5 a.m., my grandfather would get up and go make some coffee. We had this old stereo system with big speakers in the record player. My grandfather would always make his coffee and go sit right there between the record player and a wall heater whenever we would get up. We would always like to push him around through the house, although it wasn't a big house. We would roll him around through the house, and sometimes we will get on his lap, and he would roll us around.

In the evening whenever he goes to take a nap, we would take the wheelchair and push each other around. We also would fold it down and play merry-go-round on it. We would sit in the center of the tire, and spend each other around really, really fast until we got dizzy. Most days my grandfather would have company come over and hang out with him. I called them a bunch of old guys because I didn't know many of their names. Those days, those old folks didn't let kids be all in their business. One of the guys had something wrong with his feet. Both used to turn in towards each other, and he used to walk with a cane. He, along with two other guys, would come over all the time. They would sit in the living room and I would always have go to my mom's bedroom whenever they come over. My grandfather used to speak Cajun French, so sometimes whenever he would be talking,

I didn't understand what he was saying. But I think he did that with his friends because he didn't want us to know what he was talking about. They would have some awfully weird conversations. I would hear them say things when the door would creep open like *'come on in, have a seat, and get you some wine.'* To me, as a little girl, that was quite creepy. After few years, I did pick up on some of the Cajun French that he spoke. It worked in my favor for school some years later. My grandfather's favorite drink was White Port.

He'd always given us a shot in the cap every now and then. He would tell us that it will help keep away the worms. Every time he would crack open a new pint, we will take a shot. He used to go visit his family back in Midland and go on Louisa Street. Anytime he would go, he tells my mom *'I got to take my Lil Nit with me.'* We used to have a lot of fun over there and I got to play with my cousins. It was a bunch of us, but we used to have a good time. No one fighting or fussing. It was nice. We would be outside on the screen porch because it would be freezing inside the house. There wasn't a time that I don't remember going over there that it was never cold. I especially love going over there during the time when the fair came, because it was always behind their backyard. We would get up early to go over there, eat some burgers, and then head on to the fair.

There was never a time that it was a dull moment. I can say that the first few years of my life, it was great to know my grandfather. He used to tell a lot of stories. He talked about how he used to work in the field making pennies and how he only made it to elementary school. He told me how he used to work with the people at the big houses and about his ancestors from Texas. He also told me about how this white family took him in after the passing of his parents.

I was so young. As I got older, I couldn't quite remember a lot of things that he said. Only a few things stuck with me. I would sometimes have flashbacks thinking about those times and concentrating on the things that he said to me. Those are things I hold on to occasionally whenever I'm feeling down. Sometimes it's almost as if his presence is near because I would hear the squeaking of his wheeling chair rolling by.

I will never forget the words that were being said by my little brother late one evening. I can never get the image, or the cries in the room, out of my head. It was just like an ordinary morning. My grandfather would get up, as usual, go make his coffee, and back his wheelchair up between that stereo system and the heater. My brother and I would be in the bed sleeping, and sometimes my brother would get up in the morning with my grandfather and have coffee with him, then go back to bed.

It was September 18th, my cousin's birthday, but also the day before my baby brother's birthday. This particular morning, my brother would get up to have coffee. But instead of having coffee, he would find my grandfather on the floor. I was awakened to screaming. Didn't know what was going on. I jump out of bed and see my dad lifting my grandfather. He put him in the bed, and I heard my mom say he had taken his last breath. I asked what you mean? She's like he's gone. My brother said, he's gone where? They said, we must wait for the doctor to come and pronounce him dead.

I didn't know what I was experiencing. They took my grandfather out and he was never coming back. So much had happened and went on that day. I guess they were working out arrangements, and whatever my mom had to deal with, that we almost forgot it was my baby brother's birthday. He was supposed to have a party that weekend, but those words he spoke were heartbreaking. He asked mom if his papa was coming and would he be there for his birthday, and my mom said no; and we all just cried.

Even now, as I write this, it hurts. It brings back so many memories and I can't even hold back my tears. This was the first time I had experienced a loss and I didn't know how to deal with it. I had a lot of questions and no answers to them. Life as I knew it stopped. All those fun things would come to an end, only to open a chapter of my life I would have never seen coming.

CHAPTER 3

3

SEXUALLY ABUSED

I am about 12 years old at this point and my dad is outside chilling with friends and other family members. They are drinking, smoking, and having a good old time while we are in the house playing or running around outside in the backyard. Not too often I would see my dad come inside. Only to check a pot if he was cooking or to use the restroom, but his friends would come in. And you always have that one that would be brave enough to see how far he can go with me. The first time this guy comes in, he speaks and smile. This happened for several weeks. Then he started coming over at night. Went from a few days a week to every day. He would ask for a hug and a friendly hug became rubbing on my butt...to telling me sorry, it was an accident. I'm saying, how many accidents can you have?

Just blame it on being drunk. Omg, he used to stink of alcohol! Then there would be times when he would be angry. This one in particular time, it was late and they had been drinking and smoking for hours. He came in and went to the restroom as usual. Then he would come over where I'm sitting and rub his hand on my thighs and say *'I'm going to the store, do you want anything?'* I would say no because I already had snacks, and he said okay and went back outside.

He wasn't out there even five minutes and he came back in and sat down beside me again. He asked me to hold a conversation and start feeling on my legs. I felt uncomfortable, so I asked him to stop. He grabbed my legs real tight and he said *'no, I'm not doing you anything.'* I told him he was hurting my leg and one of my little brothers ran in from outside, so he got up and left. But it wasn't long before he came back once he realized the coast was clear again. He came back with a nasty attitude and asked *'why you feel like I'm doing you something? What did I do to you, huh?'* All I can do is stare at him. I had no clue to what was going on. Earlier that day I heard an argument outside, so I wasn't sure if it was a result from that or maybe it was because he was drunk. I don't know, but what I do know is he came back on the side of me and he said *'all I was doing was rubbing on your leg and you better not tell on me. Do you understand?'* And the whole time while he's telling me not to tell, he has his hands up my shorts. I didn't know what to say, how to feel, or anything. I was nervous and scared. And just when I thought I was safe because my dad walked in, he told my dad that he was just telling me about something on television.

My dad was too drunk to even realize if anything was going on. He walked in, went to the bathroom, came out and went right back outside. And as he continued telling my dad about the television show, he got up and walked out the door with him, then turned around and gave me this look like *'love, if you tell, you going to get it.'* Before he left that night, he made sure that the coast was clear just to come in and tell me *'you know, if you tell what I did, your daddy not going to believe you and he just going to whoop you.'* I was as nervous as I could ever be, I don't believe he came over for like 2 or 3 days. I guess he just wanted to see if I was going to tell or something. I didn't know what to say and was scared. By not speaking up the first time only opened more doors and opportunity for him. He came back over and realized that by me not telling, that was his way in. He went from rubbing on my thighs to rubbing on my butt, then to touching my breast here and there, then from touching all over me to showing me his private. I felt like his play toy. When he felt like playing with me, he would.

STOLEN VIRGINITY

Then here comes along another one of my dad's friends. This time it wasn't sitting on no one's lap. He pretends to dance with me because there was always music playing at our house. He takes his hand and put it in my pants and rub on me. This would happen throughout the night whenever they would be over. Every time he had an attempt to go to the bathroom, he made an attempt to come to play with me and only lasted up to a few seconds to 3 minutes. Then he'll go right back outside laughing it up as if nothing happened.

The only reason why they would run off was because my little brothers would be running around in the living room or throughout the house. See, I didn't have my own room. We lived in a four-room house. Not a four-bedroom house. A four-room, meaning we had a living room, one bedroom, a kitchen, and a bath.

The sofa was my bed. So, I really didn't go to bed until 2 or 3 a.m. most weekends because these guys were in and out of the house. I was glad when they got really, really drunk because they would pee outside or pass out to the point of having to go home. Sometimes they would sleep it off a bit then my dad would drive them home. I never looked at it as if they were watching out to make sure they wouldn't get caught, but I was bribed with candy when I was younger and they told me *'don't tell my mom or dad. You know you ate that candy, and if they find out you had all that, you can be in trouble. So let's just keep that between me and you.'* So of course, I don't want to be in any trouble. So I don't tell. I felt stupid because sometimes they gave me that candy in front my dad, so he knew I had it.

This happens for a very long time and as often as possible whenever they would be there. Sometimes it wasn't an everyday thing. Sometimes it was only on weekends. But the days they were there, it happened repeatedly every chance they got when they came in the house, and I was alone. There were always times when my mom was never at home and I was there with my dad. I remember one of the worst days of my life. I was very upset about something that happened between me and my cousin, and my dad had a bunch of guys over. They would all be in the driveway drinking. I remember trying to talk to my dad about what happened, and he blew me off. A few minutes later, one of the guys came in and ask if I was ok. I said no, because I was very upset. He said *'I can make you feel better',* and he gave me a hug and asked my brothers to go outside and play. He said that I was a big girl and they was too little to listen to what he needed to talk to me about. Once they left, he picks me up and gave me a big hug, then kissed me and said *'it's going to be ok, I'm coming right back.'* He then goes outside, and a few minutes later, comes back and asks me to sit on the bed, and told me it's ok. I was so nervous as he began to touch me and kiss me, and says *'let me see that pretty little smile of yours.'* I cracked a fake smile.

He then laid me back, pulled down my underwear, and rubbed on me while unzipping his pants. He was just looking at me while touching himself. He took his fingers and played between my legs, rubbing back and forth, trying to slip his fingers inside me and telling me to open up my legs, and that I was tight. Then he puts his fingers in his mouth, and said I tasted good. My heart is racing so fast that I start to feel my heartbeat everywhere. I thought that was weird. I tried to get up and he snaps at me quickly saying *'you better not move'* while pinning me down, and then quickly said he was sorry. Omg, I was so scared! I was saved by the laughter, I quickly got up, and he grabbed me and said *'your dad don't care, so if you tell him he's going to whip you're a**. I just* *wanted to make you feel better. When you get older you will know what to do and I can teach you how.'* I was afraid of him since, I wasn't just afraid because he was touching me; I was afraid because of the look in his eyes. It was a look I never seen before. Only if eyes can talk!

I later found out that he sent my dad and brothers to the store and he said he was going to watch me. I'm glad the store was walking distance. Who knows what could of happen if they were gone longer. A part of me wanted to get caught and just take my lick. I didn't care. I caught a whipping for nothing everyday anyway. This time I was thinking it was going to be worse, I had thoughts like *he's going to kill me!* I was nervous, scared, and feeling all types of ways.

Every time I would see him come over, I would run, and I made sure I was near somebody; but it didn't always work. He would just want to touch me or make me look at his private area, even had me touch it a few times. He would force my hand open to grab it outside of his pants or stick my hands in his pants. He would catch me and pin me up against the wall, pull me up on him where we are in a position he is good with, so he could grind on me. He would say *'be still and fix your face'*, kissing on my neck with his wet lips, and he stunk of liquor! I was even told I wasn't holding it right, and if I don't hold it or touch it the way he like, he would grab my arm and shake me until I cry, then say *'shut the f*ck up before someone hear you. I'm not doing you're a** nothing.'* At that age, I didn't know much about sex no more than from what I heard. I never had sex or knew what it felt like. When these guys come up on me and start asking me questions about me having sex, I was clueless, saying to myself that if this is sex and it is as good as I'm being told, then why it don't feel good to me.

I started having these feelings where things were happening to me after they were done, and I would be all wet. Clearly to I know what it is. They played with me so much that when I wasn't given them the satisfaction they were looking for, 2 fingers became 3 or 4, then to oral...wanting to rub their penis on me and put the head in to just 2 strokes to a few more pumps, and finish off in the bathroom.

Mouths stink of alcohol, and thinking that it was licking on me gave me chills, I felt so nasty! I would take hot baths. My water would be so hot to the point that my skin would feel like it is coming off. During my bath one night, I started to bleed. I was scared. I put a towel between my legs and went to bed. I hid it for 3 days because it wasn't so bad, but the pain was! I never told anyone until it happened again at school the next month. I found out it was my period. I thought it was a result of them putting their hands inside me.

Just when you think things can't get worse, it did. Here comes a cousin pulling the same crap; feeling on my breast, calling me pretty and beautiful, and trying to bribe me and touching me. Telling the same story...*please don't tell, you going to be in trouble, your daddy going to be mad at you, and you know how he gets when he gets mad, and you know he said he's going to whoop you if you do something you're not supposed to.* Apparently, I wasn't supposed to be doing that and it was grounds for whipping, right!

Okay, so I forgot to mention that I was called a badass sometimes, so I got a whipping like every day. On the real, I didn't think I was bad, but I was easily manipulated, yes! So, I would find myself getting caught up in things that were wrong. Like standing and jumping off the apartment stairs in our yard, or doing things with my favorite cousin that was apparently wrong. Come to think of it, everything we did was wrong in their eyes.

I saw it as having fun. We didn't have half the things kids have today. My grandfather wheel-n-chair was our car, and if we would lay it down off the floor, the tire became a merry-go-round. We would spend each other around until we got dizzy. We used an ice chest and a 4x4 board as a see-saw, and tire and rope for a swing...not to mention a rim off a bike for a basketball goal. It was fun to us, but it was wrong. So, an a** whipping we got. I was trying to avoid that every chance I got. Many times, I was like, *I* *don't even care if I tell, but if I did would they stop? Who would believe me, my drunk dad or my mom who's always gone trying to handle business?*

I grew up with boys mostly. There were hardly any girls that I played with, so I was tomboyish. Often, I wished I was a boy. I wanted to dress like them and all. I just liked their style. Besides, I hated dresses, and those damn dresses was easy access to those perverts messing with me anyway. I would be outside in the yard playing while one of my dad's friends would call me inside and say that my dad wanted me to do something. So I would go to the house to go do what I was told. I would run inside because if he called a second time after, I would be in trouble, so no questions asked. I would go inside to go do what was asked of me and he will follow me.

I swear I'm not sure if the guy friends to my cousin and my dad's friends knew that each other was doing those things to me, because it was like they were taking turns. Whenever they were out there together all the nights, they'll be out there together getting drunk and getting high from smoking weed, and just like I said, my dad is outside with the rest of his friends laughing and having a good time. The only time he would come inside was if he had to check a pot or use the restroom sometimes. He wouldn't even come in to use the restroom. They would just use the bathroom on outside the house as if it had an outside toilet out there. Well, it kind of did, but they never walked to the backyard just behind a car or something. The apartments we had in our yard had an outside toilet under the stair case for the tenants living there.

Not to mention I have seen these guys' private areas so many times, and I was asked to touch it, hold it, or just rub on it. At one point and time I thought about how disgusting it looked and I started to get angry and mad, and wondering why they are making me do this. None of this was acceptable. But now it was just going too far. While holding it one time, I started to squeeze as if to take it off. That fool said, *'oh yes, do it again harder and faster!'* I thought to myself, *what I got myself into? This is not right at all.*

I want to tell, but how can I when all I do is cry? Because I'm scared that if I tell, I'm going to get a whooping or be grounded. I won't get any snacks, couldn't go outside and play, and those were the things that meant the most to me. And if I get all those things taken away, then I wouldn't have anything. At some point, I was like I don't care if I get my snacks taken away! I don't care if I can't go outside! I just was in so much fear of being in trouble by my mom for not saying anything and catch a whooping by my dad, that I just didn't say anything.

I thought about all the times I spent in the corner on my knees on rice or getting a switch off the tree. I would find the smallest ones thinking the smaller, the better. Joke was on me! I got my a** tore up with that little switch! If not that, a wet belt. I often wondered if I did anything right. In those days, if mom whipped my a**, dad came home and also whipped my a**.

As I got older, I thought to myself, *wtf was I thinking worried about any damn snacks and playing*? If you grew up as I did, maybe you might understand why those things meant so much to me. Outside was the only activity I had, and those snacks wasn't an everyday thing. So, it was all I had to look forward to outside of everything else. When I thought about how I caught a whipping for nothing, I could only imagine what I would get if I had told, or for lying apparently.

I wasn't known for telling the truth either, according to my dad. He even had me lie to my mom about people being over at the house and even about taking the little allowance we had. All these things that happened to me happened repeatedly for a few years until eventually they stopped hanging out and stopped coming over; and when they went away, that's when it stopped. At least it stopped with them, but it wasn't near over.

STRUGGLE OR SURVIVE

When you get to the point of thinking everything's going to be ok, you tell yourself it will and you try to make yourself believe it. Despite all the things, my mom raised us to be the best that we could be to our abilities. We came up poor, but always had clothes on our backs and a roof over our heads and food on the table. There were things that happened in my life growing up that I look back on now and say that I was blessed, but the world makes it seem different. All is not what it looks to be.

As for toys and bikes, we had them, but we never got anything new much. My dad worked on the garbage truck for a few years and we got things from him whenever he brought them home. We were excited to get them too. To be honest, I enjoyed the keyboard he got me because music then became my outlet for a while.

Now don't get me wrong. We got new things, but only things that mattered. For holidays and birthdays, we got new clothes and educational toys that mom could afford. Although my mom didn't finish school, she always told us she wanted us to finish and always said *'y 'all have better eyesight than me; you can do more than what I can.'* I took everything to heart. I was just an angry child inside. I could care less about school though, but I would not dare tell my mom that. Over the years, crazy things happened. What might have seemed as if it was ok to them and fun for us became a nightmare. Leaving from down the bayou one night, my dad and the rest of the family had been drinking. As usual, the kids are off doing their own thing. I did a lot of things that I am not proud of. Just stupid bad choices. Things that could of cost us our lives, hanging out in the woods and running in front of trains, throwing rocks at the trains. But that night our lives mattered.

Headed home from the bayou side, this 4-foot little 13-year-old is in the back seat of a Grand Marques screaming for her life. Car is all over the road. It is late and dark. My dad and cousin were beyond drunk and could hardly walk, yet along drive. Somehow, my dad managed to get a few miles heading back from Raceland until he got tired of me screaming and let me drive home. He pulled over and my cousin got in the back seat while he got in the passenger seat.

I couldn't reach the gas for nothing. I had to put the seat all the way to the wheel in order to reach, but now I can't see over the dash. I said I would take my chances. How hard can it be? I seen my dad drive many times, even backwards. I got this! So I looked out the window and seen the white lines. I know I must stay within those lines, so that was how I was able to drive us until we got to Percy Brown Road. I drive straight through those curves. Good thing there wasn't any cars coming. Once I got on my street, I wasn't sure if I would make it in the driveway, and one of my little brothers started screaming at me and popped me in the back of the head. When he did, I hit our house. They made a big deal over it. There was only a board hanging off that my mom been asked my dad to fix, but we were alive, and they worried about the house. Why you think I got in trouble? Some bullsh*t I said and got popped in my mouth. This is the thanks I get for saving our lives? You got to be kidding me! At least I got their drunk a**es home. It was after 10 or 11 at night and I was driving slowly because I was afraid of going in the bayou. I was just was thinking about getting my brothers and myself home.

My mom became sick and we had to go stay with our uncle. So, after school every day our uncle would pick us up and drive us to New Orleans. He never stayed in the same spot. Always moving. We went from apartments to motels every other week. Always by airports or train tracks. The noise was killing me. While there, we hardly stayed at the room. We were always dropped off at the Celebration Station. At first it was fun, then it became a way of survival. Given only $5 with 5 kids, how in the hell you want us to play games and eat for hours of being there? We mostly just watched other kids play. You get all kinds of bad thoughts in your head. You know it was wrong, but when you are hungry, what do you do? One time, some fool left the game machine open where the tickets go. Now to me that was his mess up. I looked around and got my brothers to watch, and stole a few tickets out of it. That day we feasted on candy. It may had looked like a lot of tickets, but it wasn't. The candy was high, like 50 tickets for 1 air head. That was crazy! One day I was being super selfish, and I got myself this big mug that cost 3000 tickets. I lied to my mom and said I won it. I really stole it because I stole those tickets. I broke in so many ticket machines. Took that 5 they gave us and played other games. I had to find ways for us all to have fun. At some point we started to have a great time, until it was time to eat.

We had to sneak into birthday parties. The way my mind was set up, I would be like, we just need to see one black in this party and then we can pretend we with them. But it had to be an in and out. Don't get caught. Grab you a slice of pizza, some cake, and punch, and leave. We had to stay inside to eat it because food wasn't allowed outside of that area. We would hit up a few parties a day. Most days we were there from open to 10 pm. It became very exhausting and I was sick of pizza. I was sick of it all...the traveling back and forth every day, the lying, the stealing... everything. It didn't help any at night when gun shots were going off all the time and we would be left alone at the apartment. I had to sleep with a knife under the pillow just to feel safe. We even had to run for our lives, almost got caught up between to gangs, just because we wanted to get out of the house. Because we were stuck in there all day. Was told not to come out, but what did we do? Leave anyway. Fearing for our lives, we ran until we got back inside and never came back out. I had heard about the gangs and I can hear all the shootings, but to see two rival gangs coming at each other and you're stuck in the crossfire, that's when sh*t gets real! We were happy when mom got better. New Orleans was a place to shop for me only! But not for living.

CHAPTER 4

4

BROKEN EDUCATION

I didn't care for school too much because I really didn't have any friends, but it wasn't the only reason why I didn't like school. I hated going to school because I had trouble learning, and I had trouble reading and understanding. I could hardly pronounce any words, so I would be embarrassed when called upon to read or I would not raise my hand to read. I was told at an early age that something was wrong with me, and I had speech problems. But I learned when I got older that I suffer from dyslexia. In my head I can say the words correctly, but when I open my mouth to speak, it will not sound the same. Whenever I write I would spell my words backwards. Even when reading, I see the words and know what they are and skip over most of them. Please don't ask me to tell you what I've read because I wouldn't remember. Nobody explained to me what dyslexia was. In fact, I really didn't understand what it was until I got older. First and foremost, I already had trouble understanding. If you're not going to explain to me what the word means, how do you expect me to fix my problem?

I was taken out of my regular class and put in speech class 3 days a week while I was in 3rd grade. I was so frustrated in class because I could not say my words right for anything in the world, especially those dang gone 's' words or any words that sound alike. I know the difference, but when I speak, they must ask me which one I'm talking about. Even more frustrating because they did not understand what I was saying. Back at home, my mom tried to help me with my spelling words. In order for her to help me, I had to write all my spelling words down for her large enough so she could be able to see them. She would call them out to me to help me prepare for my spelling test. Now I always aced my spelling. It was one of my favorite subjects. Just don't ask me to say them. I became a great speller because of the spelling challenges we would have in class. I especially love those! I used to win a lot of them. Now on the other hand, I avoided the times I had to read them out loud. Sometimes it was a struggle when my mom didn't know a word and I couldn't pronounce it. That was bad. I had to find other ways to remember the word. Like call it like I see it and spell it that way too. If the test was about how to say it, I would not have passed. To match definition, I had to find a word that was spelled or meant the same as the word in order to remember them, but I had to see it. If I had to remember and write them, well, I can forget about it.

It can be very discouraging when you don't have anyone to encourage you, and they laugh at you when you pronounce something wrong instead of trying to correct you. I was dealing with other things happening in school. I had friends, but back then my parents were strict. I couldn't go out on the street and play with my friends. They were able to come and play in our backyard, but I couldn't leave. Elementary school was rough for me. I had trouble reading since I was in 3rd grade. I couldn't pronounce my words right, so it affected nearly all my subjects, and my GPA sucked. My mom always got on my case about doing my homework and keeping my grades up. I did enough to get by, but man I didn't like school, and at the same time I was happy to be at school because I wasn't at home being touched. And times that I was at home, I wish I was at school especially...on the weekends. It might sound crazy, like why would I want to be at school? But I hated school. I hated school because I didn't understand the lessons, and on top of that I was always being teased and clowned by mean girls or guys. It wasn't until I was in the 5th grade that I finally started to realize what I could do when it came down to my schooling.

Have you ever had your parents or someone tell you something and you didn't listen to them until you heard it from someone else? Yeah, that was me. I was one of those people! One of my cousins stepped up and he was like *'girl, education is important and if you don't get your grades up, you're not going to go anywhere in life. Is that what you want? To waste your life and not do anything with it? What do you want out of life? What do you want to do when you grow up?* I'm looking at him like, 'just get a job. That's what everybody else is doing.' He asked, *'you want to be like everybody else? No! Not long as I'm around you're not.'* I remember my mom would start fussing at me as I sat at the table having tons of homework to do. From the time I came home from school, I swear it would take me sometimes until 9 or 10 at night to finish my school work, all because I did not understand what I was doing. I was sitting at the table fidgeting, and I would draw all over my notebooks and do everything else but my homework. The crazy thing was I could draw, and no one taught me how. If I wasn't drawing, I was crying from sitting there and being hungry.

MAKE OR BREAK DECISIONS

In the 5th grade, we had this program at school called DARE. It was a program designed to keep kids off drugs. In the program, they talked about all kinds of drugs and how they were bad for you, the things they could do to you, and how they can make you sick. They also talked about alcohol and other things. Of course, in there while learning about how all these drugs are bad for you, I'm thinking back at home how my dad, cousins, and friends are on drugs.

Okay, now it got me wondering if I should tell the police. If I do, will I get taken away from my home? All the thoughts that were going through my head. All sorts of crazy things and I'm so confused, like this is going on in my house. But here I am at school and I'm learning that all these things are bad for you. But at home, I saw all these things that they're doing and I wanted to tell them that it's bad for you and you shouldn't do this. But I'm not about to get slapped in my mouth because that's one thing you don't do...you don't open your mouth about anything. You speak when spoken to, so I didn't say anything to no one at school about what was going on at home, and I didn't say anything to no one at home about what was going on at school. Although if I would have told, I wouldn't have had to be around those guys anymore touching me, but I didn't want to be the one to break our family up. Things would go on behind my mom back and she had no clue to what was going on. By my mom having impaired vision, they felt she couldn't see half of the things anyway, so they could just lie if she smelled something funny going on.

Towards the end of the program, we had to do a project and write a report. It was a contest, so I remember going home and sitting down at the kitchen table and I drew a picture of myself and my two brothers. I drew myself walking in between the two of my brothers and telling them how drugs are bad, and I wrote "drug-free" on it and did my essay. I won 1st place and got an A. Man! I was too excited! That was the first time I had gotten an A on doing something that I liked to do, and that was drawing. I took all my attention and every negative thing that was going on in my life and I started drawing it all the time. All my fears and worries were now in my art. In the 6th grade, it was the same old with the grades, and same old stuff going on at home. In English class, we had to do a project on Romeo and Juliet, and I was very interested in the story. I fell in love with that because I was able to put down what I wanted to say and what I wanted to do. So when it came down to doing the project, I got all excited...asking mom to go shopping for my dolls and buying the things that I needed to build a stage. Now the teacher was like, 'do something nice.' The project was far from simple, but I just wanted to do something and challenge myself to see where it took me, and I did. I went to the store and I shopped for the perfect Romeo and Juliet dolls. I got my posters, felt, paint, and glue...all the things I needed to make the perfect project. My mom saw how excited I was, so she did what she could to make sure I got what I needed.

I have a crazy imagination, so I wanted to be different. I worked on that project for days. Mind you that I had never built anything before, so I didn't know what I was doing. But I did it. I looked in the book at the scene from Romeo and Juliet, and built that stage just like it looked in the book...color and all. When I was done, I had to write my report. And after all my work was done, I made sure it was perfect. Once I got it to school and the teacher was like, "this is nice." I waited for days to get my grade. To my surprise, I got an A+ on both the project and the report, I was so happy. Later that same school year, I had a history report that needed to be done and my cousin stopped by to see how I was doing in school. I told him about the report and what we had to do. I remember him leaving and coming back with a bunch of encyclopedia. He said that we were going to get this done together and I was going to sit there and read these books, and then I was going to write my report from knowledge. He told me that I will not copy anything that I was reading right out the book. I'm saying to myself, 'man is he serious!' He asked when was the report due, then said well you have 2 days to complete it in spite what the teacher said. That way, if I messed up, I would have time to do it again. Boy was I mad, at that point! I wanted to refuse to do that report, but I had no choice. I was so mad that I wasted my own time playing around just sitting there not doing anything...tapping my pencil on the table or drawing. The longer I sat, the longer it took. The thought of reading encyclopedias was crazy to me.

Reading wasn't my strong point, and remembering what I read out all those books wasn't going to cut it. He must be stupid! After I played around and wasted my time, I decided to do it. I didn't have much of a choice really. Finally, when I was done, I was able to take the report to school; and just like any other test or report; you must wait to get your grade back. When I got my grade back, I had a B. I just knew that I had an A. My cousin would stop by to check throughout the week to see if I ever got the grade back. And when I did I told him what I made, and he was like "oh hell no! That's not going to fly!" So he came over to the school the next day so he could speak to the teacher. On top of the report it read, "Good job but some of the work was copied straight out the book." My cousin went to school and talked to the teacher. He told her how I sat there for hours reading and how he made me rewrite that report in my own words. That was the first time someone stood up for me and didn't take advantage of me. When I realized what I needed to do in school and for myself, I started looking at things differently. My grades got better because I was focused on getting away from home. They weren't all A or B's, but they weren't always bad either.

It wasn't always easy to stay focused. I could never go anywhere with friends, like to school dances or movies, because we didn't have the money. What my mom didn't put on bills, my dad smoked or got it taken away. My dad was robbed so many times that at some points, there was not enough money for the bills. I was angry! I didn't care about no bills! But I never understood because no one bothered to sit and talk with their children about their problems or finances. I only knew most of the stuff because of arguments or from being nosey. I ran away thinking things would be better for me, I ran away from home a few times. It played out in my head how I was going to plan what to do or where I was going to go. One day, I had just had enough!

I took off...no clothes or nothing...and I ran and ran! I got a few blocks away and was tired from running. It started getting dark and I was hoping they sent the police for me. I was going to tell everything! I didn't care if I was taken away. I was gone for 2 hours and decided to go back home and hid under the apartments back stairs. The dang mosquitoes started biting me, so I creeped back into the house to find my dad in the same d*mn spot when I left hours ago. This fool didn't even notice I was gone. One of my brothers asked me where I had been, and I said 'nowhere.'

I tried to run away a few other times, and sometimes I would just hide in the yard for hours just to see if anybody would look for me. Several times I packed my bags and took off, but after leaving I realized that I was leaving my brothers behind. I would ask myself, 'where am I going to go and what's going to happen to me?' I love my brothers and I love my mom and she never knew. But I was hurting inside and always wanted to tell her what was going on, but I didn't want to break my family up at the same time. It wasn't common for anybody to live in a two-parent household, and we had that; but even I know it wasn't right.

BULLIED TO BULLYING

Between my Junior High and High School years, I was dealing with being bullied. I was bullied just about every day, but not too many people knew about it because I didn't speak on it. I always got into arguments with the person who was bullying me. But I still didn't go home to tell anyone. My feelings would be hurt and I would be mad at the world. On top of being mad at the world, I was dealing with everything else that's going wrong in my life like trying to keep my grades up so I could get out of the house, trying to get away from the situation that was going on at my house, and trying to make sure the things that were happening to me would not happen again.

At this point, I was learning and reading up about molestation. I started looking things up about it because of a comment someone said, and I was being nosey. Growing up, I would hear 'curiosity killed the cat,' meaning that sometimes being too nosey can get you in trouble. Well, it paid off for me to be nosey and I was glad I did. I was listening to a lady say how she was touched and how she felt about it. It was like she was talking about what happen to me happened to her. I needed to know more. While doing my research, here come messy girls calling me out my name saying I think I'm better than them. Well, only if they knew what I was going through. The fact remains that I was being called out my name. That's not cute. Being called every name under the sun is hurtful and depressing, and those people standing around laughing and nobody helping you makes you feel shameful, lost, and confused.

When I was going to school each school year, there was a week when bullying would be a topic of importance, then it all goes away. The crazy thing about it was nobody seemed to care because it still happened to me and to others. I have seen others get it worse than I did. Because I didn't have the latest style, clothes, or shoes, I was treated as beneath them. They would talk about my clothes and how I looked. My clothes were clean and cute, and it was a style on my mom's budget. I didn't even care, but it still hurt. What they needed to do was stop being confused, because I can't think I'm better than them one day, and then the next day I'm not sh*t.

I remember one day I was about to get into a fight because a girl said that my shirt was ugly, and I said, "so!" She looked at me and asked, *you talking back to me?...*and started calling me all kinds of b*tches. Then she began pushing me. I was terrified over it. Now, why do I have to fight you because I said 'so' after you said my shirt was ugly? Before you knew it, the school crowd surrounded us. Not long after, we were broken up by the duty teacher. I spent 3 years at that Junior High School, and it was the worst. Running away and hiding was no longer an option. I would go to the library just to keep from seeing these girls. I would miss being outside, so I gave up hiding.

One day a fight broke out right when the school bell rang to go home. This one girl started picking with another student. I don't know what for. All I know is she was calling her names and pushing her. Then she proceeds to say, "B*tch get off me." I looked at her and said 'nobody on you.' I was with one of my BFFs. She looked at me and we laughed. But I just knew I was next. At some point, you must help others, and that was my first time standing up for someone. But I didn't even know what that meant at the time.

I had this one guy who would tease and call me names so much, until finally one day on way home, I was like that's enough! I will no longer let him call me out my name anymore! So I said to myself, *the next time he says something to me, it's on!* Going to school the next day, I walk down the hall. And as you know, he's there teasing and clowning me. Before you knew it, I went off! I had had enough! I called him and his friends everything that I could possibly think of. Every bad word that can possibly come out, I said it. I let him and his friends have it so bad that I hurt my own feelings. I was angry, and I had enough! I ran into the girl's bathroom stall and cried. To make matters worse, I see my friend's name written on the door of the stall that I ran into and it read that she was a H*e. I am in this bathroom and I am screaming and screaming, pulling my hair like this can't be life! Who hates me so badly, and why? I had never done anything to no one! I'm nice and I stay to myself. And why didn't anybody hear me screaming? I could hear girls come in laughing and walk out. Some came in talking, then leaving out and nobody came to see where I was. Or to even see who was making all the noise.

I didn't even go to class when the bell rang. It was all in my head and there were silent screams. I'm screaming from top of my lungs, but only I can hear myself. I got myself together and waited to go to my next class. Nobody cared, so I no longer didn't. Every day after that, before anyone of those boys got a chance to tell me anything, I would just go off. I finally had enough! What did I do wrong and why did I feel bad? I just did the same thing to them that they were doing to me. Then I found out that one of those boys liked me and I wouldn't give him the time of day. That still didn't give him the right to do what he did. He was in special education, so I used that on him. I called him dumb, stupid, and retarded. Even got in his face a few times. It was bad enough that I was cheated on by my boyfriend because I wouldn't sleep with him, I had my reasons, and yes it was because I was afraid to. Not because of getting pregnant or anything, but because I knew better and I had taking parenting skills, child development, and other classes that talked about prevention. Everything I did was for a purpose, and as for that purpose, I didn't sleep with him. Now I had the knowledge about sex, but I was still confused about what had happened to me when I was young. How can you read about something that's supposed to be intimate between two people of age, but then you know those things that happened to you were not consented between two people, and one not of age?

CHAPTER 5

5

BROKEN TRUST

I didn't have many friends, and the girls I was very close to I could only see during school. I had made friends with my neighbor's kids. They were younger than me, but that was cool. I loved hanging out over at their house. Every chance I got I would hang over there. Their mom was cool, and I could just go talk to her a lot about things. Her sister's kids used to come over a lot and I became friends with them as well. Something happened one night that changed my relationship with them, and we never spoke again. That night replays over and over again in my head. Not only did I lose friendships behind this, but I lost members of my family. Some things you just don't understand, or try to figure out why people do the things they do. Still, till this day I never got an apology. Man, it still hurts.

I talked about my favorite cousin a bit...the one I got in trouble with as little kids. Well, her mom was super cool, but she would talk about my cousin sometimes because she would get herself into trouble a lot...even got locked up a few times. I hated seeing my cousin like that. I hated hearing her mom say things about her. She even told me we should change places because she was so bad. I felt like she blamed things on her just because I don't know, but this time she wasn't here to blame her. What I found out later shocked the hell out of me.

It's November...football season. I used to help my uncle write names on the football boards sometimes. I had been doing since I was like 12 or whatever. The people that were there were his regulars. I already knew what squares they had and how many they want. I would put team names and number them sh*t. I ran them boards, he just collected the money, but I still got paid. I used to run 2 or more boards at a time. $2.50, $5.00, even $1 boards. On Thanksgiving, he would have $10 and $25 boards. Well, this happened to be a Thanksgiving board. It was a big game. I remember doing a few boards over the course of a few weeks, and I remember my cousin being on a few. On the night of the big game, they were chilling at my house and us kids just running around. I'm back and forth from my house to the neighbor's house.

Mom had cooked a big meal and asked me to wash the dishes. While doing so, my cousin was in the kitchen arguing with her husband over money for cigarettes. She kept telling him no, but he wasn't having no for an answer. At some point during halftime, her and my mom left and came back. She was all happy. She had won $50, flashing a $50 bill. Her husband was still bugging her and I guess she gave in. I go back by the neighbor's house. While there, something unusual happened.

My cousin came over there. That was strange to me because, all the times she had been over by mom's house and the neighbors been staying there, she never came over to visit. Hardly said two words to them. What was different this night? At this point, they always played special commercials doing these games. I don't know what was playing, but it was the funniest one yet. The neighbor's daughter and I were laughing so hard that we had tears rolling. Who would have known within 5 minutes after I would be crying real tears? I see my cousin call my friend's mom over and they stepped inside the bedroom by the living room. The door was half open. I couldn't hear what was being said, but I see this look in their eyes now. I was still laughing at the TV. I read the lips of my friend's mom. When I turned and looked inside the room, and it seems as she said "NO, not Nitra!" My friend's mom had this disappointing look on her face and my cousin walked away and went back to my house. Not long after, I was called back home, but the look on the face of my friend's mom was really disappointing.

I was met at the door with a belt. My mom and my cousin were like "where it at?" I'm like, *where what at?* My mom said, "Well I'm not going to ask you again!" I'm like, *what are you talking about?* She was like, "oh so now you playing stupid? Not going to ask you again!" I began to cry. I didn't know what's going on. Before I knew it, I was being embarrassed. I was searched and had all my things searched, but that was not the embarrassing part. It was when I was asked to pull my pants down and getting my underwear checked. Like wtf! If you could only imagine what's going on in my head. I'm crying my eyes out and still don't know why. After they didn't find anything, they proceeded to tell me that my cousin won $250 on the pool. So I'm like, ok what that got to do with me? And wait, how? She came in here flashing $50. How 50 goes to 250? Help me understand! And what does that have to do with me? I was asked, "did you take it?" I'm like, how? I didn't even know she won $250! I do know she was on the $50 board. After the numbers are pulled, I couldn't care any less who wins. I never see any of the money. I just did what was asked of me and I get paid whatever my uncle gives me for helping him. I was hurt, and I went off. I was like, how in the f*ck you going to come at me with this bullsh*t?! I never stole anything from you! I got my a** tore up after being slapped in the mouth. I was embarrassed by pulling my pants down in the living room instead of bringing me to the bathroom. Come on now!

You see, before this night I would go to the store for my cousin to buy her cigarettes, and she would give me 20s...even hundred-dollar bills sometimes, and she would tell me to buy whatever I wanted. Mom would tell me to bring the money back and let the person give me what they could afford, and then I go back to the store and buy what I wanted. I always did that. I told her that and she was like, "you are right, but I can't find it and who else could have taken it?" Well there was a number of mother f*cking people walking all up in there, but it wasn't me. Back then kids were able to buy alcohol and cigarettes. But the people at the store knew who you were. I never took anything from her, and for her to accuse me of stealing?! The nerve of her! The only time I stole was to eat years ago when we were left. I knew then that was wrong, and was scared to death of being caught. And before that and beyond that, I never stole anything else ever again. Later that night, my mom gets a call from my cousin's husband, and he said that she had put it in the car. He apologized to my mom for what happened, but it was behind something dealing with the adults and I was good bait. It wasn't anything for someone who had lots of money to feel sorry for somebody else, and to just offer the money to them just because.

When my mom found out, she told me sorry. The friendship between my mom and cousin was no longer. They were like sisters' best friends that bullsh*t broke up our family, it was never the same. All behind a man and some money who would later turn out to be nothing in my eyes. My cousin was my mom's deceased sister's daughter, and they are the same age and were the best of friends. Just so sad how their relationship ended. I just wish my mom believed me before I was embarrassed like that. My little cousin was my BFF, and we were now separated. I don't even think she knew what happened because she was locked up at the time. Still til this day, I wonder if she was ever told what happened. A few days later, I went by my friend house and everyone started treating me differently. I don't know what she told them, but whatever she said it sure did turn them against me. After a while, they just stopped talking to me. I guess they thought I was a thief and wanted nothing to do with me. They never stopped to think that the few years they knew me, I never took anything from them, nor gave them a reason to think that I was that type of person. I still spoke with the mom and her daughter every now and then, but that later ended.

Not long after, something tragic happened one night to the mom. I remember being over at the house and everyone was happy. It was late and I had just returned home and went to bed. I could hear screams. Woke up to flashing lights all over, and the booming sounds of knocks at our front door. I slept on the sofa every night and flashing lights wasn't anything new on our streets. This time our living room was lit up. I looked outside and saw police everywhere, and everything was blocked off. The sight was disturbing, and there was blood everywhere from the house to 7 houses down, with chunks hanging off the fence. I thought I was dreaming. I wish I was. It was really bad, but thank God she lived.

My life was changed because of people I thought cared for me. It's one thing to get bad reactions from strangers, but for family to pull that crap to a child?! Man, all I could think about was how my cousin did me wrong and embarrassed me. I hated her and never talked to her again. When I see her now, I speak only because I have forgiven her and because it's the right thing to do But I have nothing else to say behind it. I became cold-hearted. I never showed anyone what I was thinking. I smiled when I needed and kept it moving. If anyone came at me wrong, I was letting them have it. I started bad-mouthing people with cussing. And so that I wouldn't get in trouble, I knew a girl who spoke French who taught me a few bad words, and I started using them. I had this 'I don't give an F*ck' attitude.

Life had to be better than this. I come from being poor, not knowing how to read, being molested, teased about my clothes, and watching my brother come up to get beat and picked on because of his eyesight. Oh my God, man this is crazy! Things at home weren't any better, and I got into it with my family every day before and after school. I had nowhere to turn or no one to trust.

CHAPTER 6

6

MENTALLY BROKEN

H ave you ever been told that you're not going to amount to anything? Or that when you grow up, you're going to be a h*e? I was told that I was going to have all these babies with no man to help me take care of them, I was going to be a dropout, and that I was pretty; but that's all I was good for and that somebody was going to take advantage of me. How do you come back from all the bad things that have been said and happening to you constantly over and over again? And just when you think it's getting better, the sh*t hit you in the face again? By the time I was turning 16, I was so lost and still no one knew what was going on in the inside of me. I was so hurt and so full of pain, but at the same time I had joy for other things. How can you have a love and hate for the world at the same time? I hate the world because all these things that were going on that were bad, but I love the world because of the beauty that you could see in it.

By this time, my mom and dad had a divorce and we were now living in two different homes, going back and forth. I thought my dad didn't want us, because every time the weekend came and it was time to go to his house, he would never show up to pick us up. But his sister would pick us up and we were staying over at her house until he got in. He was telling us lies, saying he was going to take us shopping and do all these amazing things; and it would never happen. We would wake up the next morning and that man would be gone. Where? No one knows. This happened weekend after weekend after weekend. We would end up sleeping over at our grandmother's house and I would be afraid because while everyone's asleep, someone always sneaks into the room. It would be dark, so dark that you cannot see anything at all; but someone would stand there and watch. Sometimes I thought I was tripping, like I was hallucinating thinking something was wrong with me again. I didn't tell anyone because I thought they were going to think that I was a freak. One night, someone came in, covered my mouth, and started touching and rubbing all on me; and rubbing his penis up against my body. I'm saying to myself, 'this can't be happening again!' It got to the point that I started accepting what was happening to me. If I knew it was going to happen, I would find ways to cope with it. Since my family on my dad's side love to drink, there was always alcohol around all day every day.

Alcohol wasn't anything new to us, but we would take a few beers and go drink it. They wouldn't even know because they were so drunk. So I began drinking and getting drunk, so that if something would have happened to me, I wouldn't feel it much, and I sure in the hell didn't want to remember it. I just wanted to be numb. I was robbed out of everything that was meant to be good, and there was no use trying to wait and see if anything was going to change. My life was pointless. It sure wasn't mine anymore. At some point, I began to drink all the time whenever I would be over there. No one would knew about it. I mean my brother would have a drink with me too, but I wouldn't even know what was going on. I covered up so much and kept anyone from knowing what was going on with me that I didn't know what was real anymore. When I was little, they said I would lie when I didn't, but now I did. Sex was overrated to me and I wanted to sew up my vagina. I read about molestation and was always told to not say anything, but I knew it was okay and right to say something. I was just too ashamed at that point to say anything, so I allowed this to keep happening to me. Alcohol became a part of my life and it helped me cope with what I was dealing with. Somehow, I lost myself and didn't know who I was anymore, I felt like my life didn't belong to me. It was for anyone who wanted a piece of me to do as they pleased, and I allowed and accepted it. Deep down, I felt guilty as if I had done something and was hiding it. I was afraid of the dark and tired. Someone please tell me how to end it!

I also always felt that our family did not accept us. Because we didn't live near them, we were treated differently, and I didn't like it. I finally got to the point where I was like, *you know what, I'm not going to do this anymore. I'm not coming back here!* So I told my mom that it was pointless for us to go to my dad when he was never there. So I decided to stay home. After a while, I was able to decide whether or not I wanted to go see my dad because I was the oldest. And because my brother was so much younger, I started developing a bad relationship with my baby brother. It became my fault that he wasn't able to be around his dad, I tried explaining it to him, but it's like he would never understand where I was coming from. I started thinking that was the reason why he started acting the way he was acting and doing the things he was doing at school. Our relationship never got better. It only got worse, but I always still trying to help him whenever I could. Still, until this day, I never told him why. And whenever I try, I feel like anything I say goes in one ear and out the other. When life comes and hit you like a Mack truck and you have nothing left to give, you find yourself in a place that you don't want to be. For months, all I had been thinking about was how could I stop these things from happening to me constantly. It was driving me insane and I didn't know what to do.

My mind was racing a hundred miles an hour. I'm thinking about everything that has gone wrong and everything that happened. Why would they say I will not amount to anything? Why would people take advantage of me? Why would they call me dumb? Why would they say I would never finish school? It seemed as if all odds were against me. I thought about ways how I could just say *forget it, it's not worth it! I'm not worth it and this can't be life!* On the outside people saw me smile but, in the inside, I felt like everything in me would just rip apart. I'm in the crowd of people and I no longer want to be there because I'm afraid of what they might think of me. As if everyone knew my secret. Hearing them saying 'you sh*t you, you are getting what you deserve! You are such a loser, you never going to be sh*t!' I'm screaming, *make it stop! Please!* I would go off to myself and cry. But the minute someone comes around, I'd pretend that nothing was wrong. Have you ever been in a room that's full of people, but you feel like you're the only one there? You can see people talking, but you don't hear them. Like you're stuck. Everything around you is moving and you are not. I thought about all the possible things that I could do to myself. I thought, *who would miss me if I'm gone?* I thought about all those things, about ways that I could end it all. I got to the point where I was tired...tired of pretending it's ok, tired of being the strong one, tired of being used. But then the voice in my head says no, it shall get better. I thought about the things that were said to me and wonder about them, when I was told I was beautiful, and I was worth being told that I was beautiful. I want to feel special, but how could I allow myself to be special.

BROKEN HEART

My mom was often gone a lot, so I hung out at my aunt's house, who also happens to be my Godmother. She didn't have kids, so she spoiled me. I didn't have to go far because she lived in the same house. Almost only one wall separated us. Our house and hers were back to back, I would just walk out my door and walk to the back of my house. She was great, and everyone thought she was my mom. She used to work over at the hotel, and on paydays, she would bring me on her job. And then we would go ride around to the stores and I got to get any kind of snacks I wanted. She had a big piano in her living room she used to play. I can only remember her teaching me how to play Mary Had A Little Lamb. She used to enjoy music, especially that Electric Boogie song...the one by Marcia Griffiths that said "It's electric, Boggie woogie, woogie!" That was her favorite. I could hear that song playing every time I think of her.

She told my mom that I was old enough to go to the store on my own. At some point, she got hurt and had to go to the back and neck clinic twice a week. I hated seeing my aunt in pain, but we would still walk across that bayou and back. After she would be done with her therapy at the clinic, we would go to Popeye's and get biscuits, 3 for $1 with grape jelly. Sometimes we would stop at the wig shop to look at new wigs. Boy did she like her wigs! We used to talk a lot about things. When I first got to Junior high school, she would be the first one up in the mornings. I knew when it was time to get up because I could hear her close and lock her front door. She would walk alongside the driveway and come in our front door, walk to the bathroom, and play in her hair. Once done, we had 3 chairs that would be stacked in the living room right by the front door. She would sit there until I got on the bus. She did that every morning. One Friday night, my mom and my stepdad wanted to go to the trailer that he had. We would go there on some weekends where all the kids could get together, or we all got together as a family. My stepdad had a daughter and 3 sons. He had another daughter, but she was older and didn't live in the area. For the most part, we all got along. There was a lot of times things happened that I didn't approve of so, I stayed to myself. I was still the oldest out of the kids, which I hated sometimes.

One weekend, I didn't want to go. I didn't know why. I cut up. I was so mad at my mom. I wouldn't talk to any of them. She said, "you never asked to stay home before. Why now?" My stepdad was like, "you just wanted to stay home and go be with boys." That wasn't true. I really didn't know why I wanted to stay. I just knew that I did. I don't know if by me not staying was a good thing, or if I have stayed would've turned out to be bad for me. That next morning, we are at the trailer and I got up still not talking to anyone. I didn't even eat breakfast. I was mad. When I get mad, I go for days without talking sometimes. I went to the room I shared with my stepsister. I don't know what for, but when I walked back down the hallway, I felt this sharp pain in my chest. Like somebody stabbed me fast, then pulled the knife out. I went and told my mom about it. She asked if I was still feeling it, and I told her no. She told me to go lay down for a while. I did, and the pain had gone away as fast as it came. I ended up taking a nap. When I woke up not long after, I felt the pain again, this time much worse than the first. It came then left, never happening again. Later that evening I'm walking back down the hallway and I look out of the window and see a car pull up. It was another one of my mom's sisters with her husband. Now she has never come over to our trailer while we were there before. What makes this time different?

I see her and her husband get out the car and my mom walk out the door. The look that was on my auntie's face wasn't right. At this point, I'm still in the house. I see my mom go walk towards her. By the time my mom can reach her, I just knew something was wrong. I could read the looks on their faces. They started talking and I could see my mom's head go down, then she turned and walked towards the house. I just broke down and started crying because I knew right then that something was wrong. As my mom made it to the door and came into the house, I just started screaming. No! It can't be! I heard what she said, but I didn't want to accept it. I had a million questions going on in my head. Like how? And why? We had packed our things up and headed back home to Thibodaux.

67

Now for some reason, I don't know why, but I was scared to go inside the house. I had this feeling before about being scared and afraid to be inside the home. What was this feeling I was feeling? I didn't understand it. Nobody had time to tell me anything. I went and sat in the living room in the big chair, and I just stared at the pile of chairs that was by the front door that my aunt would sit in every morning before I went to school I was just wishing she was there. She is usually the one I can talk. Who do I talk to now? I didn't know how to feel at this point. I was sad because another person that I really truly cared about and felt safe around was gone.

We were told that she died of a heart attack. I thought they tried to keep information away from me, but ever since I was a little kid, I've always been nosey; so I try to listen in on their conversation from time to time and I overheard them saying something that sounded someone had broken into the home and scared her. That may have been the cause of the heart attack. I don't know if anything was missing or anything, but I never was told anymore from that. Later that week, I sat down and had a conversation with my mom. I told her I didn't understand. She said that she died from a heart attack, and I was told around the time that she had passed was the time that I was feeling those chest pains. I was told that, because I was so close to her, I felt when she passed. That was scary! After that, I couldn't sleep for weeks. Mornings when I got up for school, I could hear the sound of her front door closing. I could hear her walking and closing our front door. She used to put on Skin So Soft lotion and perfume, I could smell the perfume in the air. I would peek under the covers to see if anyone would be there, but there was no one and it felt so real. I would see shadows passing through at the same time every day. Could you imagine how I was freaking out?

I was even afraid to go into the house when they went in to take all her things out to donate them. It was a very sad time for me. I just couldn't do it. I was walking down the street one day a few months later, and I had got over my aunt's passing. And someone walked up to me and told me, "I'm sorry for your loss." I said, "excuse me?" She said, "I'm sorry about your mom. She had passed not long ago." I didn't know where my mind was. I ran home, and I was like, what happened to mom?

Not too many people knew that my godmother wasn't my biological mom. When people would see me with my mom, they were like "I didn't know that was your mother." I really truly miss my godmother. One thing that I could say is that she kept it real with me. I wish I could have shared more of my life with her, even all my secrets.

Didn't even have a chance to talk to her about when we were together, how when she used to be inside the room during therapy, they would have this guy that passed by all the time. At first, I didn't pay it any mind. But then I started to recognize the white truck with the blue stripes. It would be on my mind to tell her, but she would come out doing better and I was happy for her, so I just kept it to myself.

It felt as if the pain I was feeling would never go away. In time it did, but before I was able to get over it, I was dealing with so many things and I just didn't know what to do or which way to turn. I started to notice that the guy in the truck would be following us every week, and he would put his hands out the window and wave for me to go to him. Now, of course, I knew better. This guy would ride in circles around the parking lot. Every week I would see him, and he started to follow us. I would start seeing him on our street. What did this guy want? He had to be in his 40s or something, and he's stalking me? He would always be watching and waiting for his chance to do I don't even know what! Over at the clinic one day, he passed by. And this time he had money in his hand. He was cruising really slowly in the parking lot. Now I'm not sure if it was windy or not that day, but the money came out his hands. Was he expecting me to go out and pick it up?

I don't know, but I do know that I wasn't any fool! Maybe I was a fool for not telling, but not a fool to give him a chance to grab me?

CHAPTER 7

7

INSULTS TO INJURY

Many people assume that abuse only means that physical violence is happening, but that's not always the case! Abuse comes in many forms. It's not just physical. Although I was physically and sexually abused, I was also verbally abused. One time when I was when my dad, he asked me if I knew where my mom had gone, and I told him no. I couldn't tell you whether he was drunk or sober that day. And to be honest, I couldn't even care. The fact remains that he beat me. He asked me a question, I gave him my answer, and he didn't like the answer I gave him. So whatever! His problem, not mine. Over and over he asked me, "where's your mom?" I would tell him that I didn't know where my mom was. I don't know! So, he got mad and beat the daylights out of me with that belt for no reason. I don't know what got into me, but immediately after he finished beating me, I just snapped. When he put the belt down, I grabbed it. I don't know the person that I became at that moment. My dad stands at least 6 feet high, and I got to swinging.

I hear him screaming at me, telling me to stop. Eventually he was able to snatch the belt out of my hand. Now what the crap I did that for? I asked for that next whipping, I guess. Any time before that, I might have just got slapped in the face or something. But he beat the sh*t out of me again. I cried after seeing all the bleeding welts on my body. Those laceration and bruises were the worse from any whippings I ever had, and lasted for days. Some of them were bloody for a while. I had bleeding welts before from tree switches and hot wet belts right out the tub, but this time it was different. The pain was unbearable. When he said he was going to give me a raw a**, he meant that sh*t. I couldn't sit down for days and had to pull my clothes off my skin from the sores. The verbal abuse came when I was being called all kinds of b*tches and h*es, and told that I would not be worth nothing. I never will understand how a person who claims to care for you can hate you at the same time. I got so used to hearing all that dumb crap that I didn't even care no more. It just became a part of who I was. Sometimes before, they could open their mouths and say what they had to say and I would beat them to it by saying, 'yeah okay I know.' It got so bad I had to get out of my mother's house. I was too embarrassed to even go to school. I was lied on, lied to, and told stories about things that other people said about me. But they never said it to my face. I was told my name was written on phone booths and said that I suck d*ck and that I am a b****, etc. Now this was almost every day.

That wasn't so bad compared to the writings on the wall. Yes, you read that right. The writing was as huge as can be! I was called b*tches before, but to see it in fluorescent paint in giant letters bold letters across your entire house?! Smdh! One time was one time too many, but every f*cking morning?! I said to myself, "no way! Who can be doing this?" I was told that it was a girl getting back at me because I took her man. What!!! First off, who in their right mind has time to get up in the middle of the night and paint bad names on another person's property? Where was the ladder and flashlight, I asked? It's dark when I get up for school, so they had to use some type of lighting to be able to see. I was told that I had to repaint the house after school, meaning that the writing stayed on the house displayed for everyone to see all day. When I got off from school, it takes me almost all the rest of the day to paint it. Just to wake up the next day and there it is again. I had to go through the whole process of that all over again. On top of getting yelled at, because whoever was ruining the house now became my fault now. This crap happened for a little over two weeks, then stopped and started up again.

I had enough of the bullsh*t, I said. I started staying up to see who was doing this. So that night, I did just that. The next morning there was nothing written on the house. The same night, I go to bed just to wake up the next morning to paint again. Smh! You are kidding me right?! So I would start going to bed early and get up like 3 am peeking out of the windows. Over the next few days, I saw no one and my mom even stayed up with me sometimes. Nothing happened for weeks. I finally go back to my regular bedtime, and what do you know?! I said no, no this can't be! This must be somebody we know who is doing this. How can they possibly know what's going on? How can they even know when I stay up or not? This is crazy! There it was again big, BOLD, bright and loud, "ANITRA IS A B*TCH!" I thought it was funny.

They had to be f*cking nuts if they thought I was going to paint this sh**. Let whoever wrote it paint it, and I went to school. I got fussed at, but I didn't care. I meant I wasn't painting it. Paint it for what? So they can continue doing it? Besides, we barely had paint left to repaint it, and I wasn't breaking any more of my sleep. I was barely keeping my eyes open in class and that couldn't fly with me. After leaving it on there for several days, it finally got repainted and there was no more writing on the house after that. So, either the person stopped and got tired, or maybe figured they won. We never found out who did it, but I always had an idea who it was.

Trying to avoid all the drama back home, I ended up getting kicked off campus every day because I was trying to stay longer just to keep from going home. I had a job, but it wasn't doing me any good. All my money went to cab fare. I caught a cab from school to home, from home to work, and from work back home. Worked 3 days a week, 4 hours a day. I wasn't getting enough hours that I needed for school for my credits. It was one thing after another. I felt my walls closing in. I couldn't talk to nobody about it. There was nobody I trusted to tell all this information to. There was one person I could talk to about the present time, but not my past. I could call him every day from the school pay phone just to hear his voice. It would put a big Kool-Aid smile on my face.

It didn't last long because one of the assistant principals would see me and ask me if I had somewhere to be? And then he would escort me out of the building I would sneak back in and go to the back of the school, trying to avoid all school administration until the bell rang.

It's one thing to be abused yourself, but to know of a child being abused a few months old? Each time I would see this child, the kid would have different bruises on their body. At this point, I'm like "yo, nobody sees this?" I would bring it to someone's attention and ask, "how do you not see this?" I never witnessed this child getting hurt with my own eyes, but it doesn't take a rocket scientist to figure out that something was wrong with the child.

I didn't know who to ask questions about what was going on with this child. I was told that it wasn't my child, so it wasn't any of my business. But I didn't care this is a baby, to be honest. It pissed me off. So I spoke up and said something about it, and I told everyone off. Finally, something was done, but at the end of the day nothing still was accomplished. They got a chance to talk to the mother after authorities got involved. There was all kinds of lies and saying this and that, and that the baby had fallen and all kinds of other bull crap. So they just let it go. It wasn't much longer until I witnessed bruising once again on this child and I spoke up and said, "Enough is enough! I no longer want to be around something so horrible." The child was living elsewhere, but the child was part of the family where I was now staying and would come over to visit. Who speaks up for this child if I leave because I was ready to go before, and I would get the blame if the child was hurt. The only reason why I was there is because I was living with the person I love. I asked myself this question, "If I leave what will happen?" I will be taking a part of myself away from someone who I truly cared for and cared for me. The only person I felt that I can trust at that time and I was just 17.

We had a long talk because I was ready to walk. I was willing to go back to the crap I was going through at my mom's rather than see a child in this condition. What do I know about anything? I would tell myself not to leave and that they will take care of it, so of course, I said I would stay. We hadn't seen the child for at least a month or two after that. When the child did come back over to visit, oh my God! It was horrifying at this point. The baby was about 8 months old and was covered with cigarette burns. What do you do at that moment that you see this? You have no clue who to tell, what to do, which way to turn. At the end of the day, it was reported and we ended up with a victory. I ended up taking on a responsibility larger than myself and I didn't know how because of all the stuff that I went through I now find myself working two jobs, trying to put myself through school, and helping take care of a child who is not mine. When you must deal with people that was willing to cover their own a** instead of doing what's right, you question a whole lot. I always question about what's right and what's wrong in this world, because I know deep down, I am a good person and I want to be different. But we can never catch a break. Now idk if it's just me, but I seriously think that we were racially profiled. They told us it was a misunderstanding. If a misunderstanding is this scary, I hate to see what the outcome would be if we truly were the one committing the crime. We don't bother anyone. We go to work and back home, and being that the love of my life and I both worked together was great. This didn't occur until after I would move out my mom's house.

We had the evenings off, and on our off days, especially pay days, we would walk over to Blockbusters Videos to get new movies and walk over to Winn-Dixie to get some food to boil. That was our thing. We didn't have a car so we would walk those 4 miles like nothing because we were used to it. Besides, we enjoyed each other's company while taking our slow walks and holding hands. We would take the same route every time. We get a few blocks away from the house and we would hear police sirens coming our direction, which is nothing new. Police were always flying around here. They were deep on the canal that night and we were engaged in a conversation. We saw them through a side street and said "man, they after somebody man!" It was like the whole force was out. We continued bout our business with no care or worries. We get a few more blocks up and police still rolling. By the time we get near our job off the side street, we hear something creeping up behind us, so we turn to see what it was because we had moved over to the side out of the road. The car wouldn't pass us and they didn't even have on lights. The minute we turned around, we were blinded by bright lights, and within like 2 seconds of that, police surrounded us. They were jumping out their cars and were like, "Put your hands where we can see them!" They were asking us what we had in our hands. We had 2 movies from the video store, nothing else. Just going return them and get some more before the store closed at 11pm.

Police had us lean up on the car, patted us down, checked our movie cases, and then told us that somebody robbed the store a few blocks away. We were coming from that way and fit the description. Then one police officer said "the black guy over there has on the exact colors and fits the description at the robbery." They asked us to get in the back of the car and drove us back to the crime scene...well not so much. They had us stand a half of block away from the store in the dark while a white couple and some other random people stood with the police talking. The police talked to them for a bit, and I'm standing over there a nervous wreck praying that they don't lie. I can barely see them, so how can they even see us in this little light from that street light that sat a few feet behind them? Well, thank God they said it wasn't us or my love. The guy that robbed the store had on black and gray, just opposite of what he had on. But there were 2 big a** differences! He's black and the robber was white. He's 1 hundred and some whatever pounds, and my baby was pushing 200. I was pissed and embarrassed because, when they surrounded us, it was by my job and the night crew was outside trying to figure out what had happened. Stuff like that can affect your job. No way I was losing mine behind this. I had got promoted to assistant manager. No way this was happening.

They had ruined my night. Then one of the black officers offered to take us to return our movies before we got a late fee. I was mad and wanted to walk, but he was like "let's just go because it was almost like starting our walk over." That store that was robbed wasn't that far from our home. Besides, I didn't want to get in the back of no d*mn police car. People were looking at us crazy when they opened up the door and let us out. I didn't even want to look for no movie. I already had this bad vibe about the police since a little girl when my mom opened up the door because of them d*mn near knocking it over and busting in. The whole force was out there with guns all up in my mom's face asking for some guy who she didn't even know...all because of the addresses being so messed up saying they were at the wrong house. Then they took off. No apologies or nothing. That could have ended badly! Again, thank God He was on our side. As far as the police, they all not bad. It's just not cool to be in the mix of something or accused by them because you just never know how the ending is going to play out.

CHAPTER 8

8

INTIMIDATION

The boy that I couldn't stand, the man that I once known as my best friend, turn superhero, turn boyfriend, turn fiancé, then turn husband somehow got me to the point where I wasn't any longer myself. It wasn't always like that. It started off bad for us trying to be together. Man, did we have some loops to jump through; but we got through. All the sh*t that I've been through, and needless to say that when we were little, I could not stand him. But somehow, through our job we became closer. When I first met him, we were little kids running around through the yard. I didn't like him that much, but we talked and had conversations from time to time, and I considered him my friend. I never knew that he was going through something because we didn't talk about that. All we did was clown around. We were in elementary school at that time, and we only hung out at home because boys and girls didn't have recess together at our school. Being that we lived on different sides of the track, we went to two different schools for junior high.

The schools would separate us for 3 years, and he was also a year older. So honestly, when I got to high school, I didn't even see him. But the fact that I needed a job for the program that I was in at school is what led us to get back together. While at work, we clowned around a lot at the same time. I started crushing on him, and I couldn't tell him that because I had a boyfriend. I had a secret boyfriend who no one knew about...not even my mom or brothers. I don't really know why we called each other boyfriend and girlfriend, because we were more like best friends...and we are still today. We only got to see each other sometimes at work and after school...only if we got 10 minutes to see each other, that's all we got. We worked right down the road from each other and he usually got off before me, so he would stop by and see me. Most of the last time I wouldn't be able to talk to him because I was busy taking calls, so he would sit there and have conversations with those that came in and out of the building. I only had enough time to give him a hug and he would tell me he was going home to do homework and get ready for school the next day. Only thing we ever did was meet on the canal and give each other a hug 5 days a week. Sometimes we didn't even see each other on weekends; but between those hugs after 3 pm and seeing each other once he get off from work for a few minutes, that was it. No kissing, no dates, no movies, no nothing.

One night when he got off from work, I told him that I had wanted to talk to him. So I had arranged for someone to take my calls while I stepped outside. I was super nervous because what I was about to do, I really didn't want to. I believe it was the first conversation that I had with someone that was kind of hard for me to break bad news to. We stepped outside, and as usual, I'm asking how his day went with school and work. I told him I needed to talk to him, and he asked me what's up. I told him that we have been dating for 2 years and the only thing we accomplished doing was to see each other at 3 pm or after 3 pm five days a week and never went on any dates or anything. I said it was just best that we stay friends. To my surprise, he agreed with that. Over the next several weeks, he was still stopping by to come see me, but that night I broke up with him. I sat in the office and had a conversation with my friend, and of course he asked me if I was okay. I told him yeah and explained to him kind of like what was going on. But he already had known because we had been talking already. It felt good to have someone in my corner. I was glad that I could call the person in my corner my friend. It wasn't too long afterwards that our friendship became more. I was really crushing on him and I know he was feeling me too, but he was acting like he was shy and didn't want to say anything. He stepped outside one night to smoke a cigarette, so I went outside with him. It was freezing out.

I asked him if I could have a cigarette and he said "you don't smoke." I said, "You don't know what I do!" It's not like I hadn't smoked a cigarette before. I had smoked several cigarettes to be honest, but I really didn't want a cigarette. I just wanted to step my game up so that I could holler at him, because I knew he was feeling me. He acted as if he didn't want to say anything, so I asked him out. He said yes and was in shock. He told me he didn't think a fine, pretty girl like me would go out with a big guy, and he thought I liked another guy there. I did, but he was old news. We had a crush on each other when he lived across the road from me. He used to buy me candy and show off by popping wheelies on his bike. His little nephew was a pain in the a**! He almost got me caught up many days screaming that I was in love with his uncle outside my window. His nephew was his sister's son. They were a few years apart. The relationship ended when they moved. I just used to clown around with him at work, that's it. I was crushing on you is what I told him. If anyone would have told me that our first date out would have been a bad experience, I never would have made any moves. Here I am grown enough to work, and I must hide a relationship from my mom and stepdad because they were going nuts. It was almost my 18th birthday and the time leading up to it was moving in slow motion. The only thing that I ever wanted was to be happy, and he made me happy.

On the first night we went out, yes, I lied to my mom and said that I had to work. But she never came over to my job before, and for some reason that night she locks her keys in the house. Out of all days, why this night? She went over to my job looking for my keys and I wasn't there. When I got back, I was told that my mom was looking for me and she wasn't too pleased to find out I wasn't there. Some of the workers who I was cool with tried to cover for me. One of them even tried calling where I was. We wanted to be alone and we saw the phone ringing. He had one of those see-through phones that lit up when it rang. There were a few calls. Now if we would have answered, I might be telling this story differently. We had been talking for a minute leading up to this night and it had been planned for about 2 weeks. We planned it on both of our off days just to be alone at his house in his room. Although it wasn't my first time, it was my first time without protection with my consent. He was the boy that turned into a man, and the only man I would sleep with over the next 20 years except the time I was raped. It was one hell of a night and that night told me everything that I thought I needed to know about my parents and how they truly felt about me. We got into a heated argument and I just didn't understand why I couldn't have a boyfriend. All the yelling was getting to me and I heard my stepdad yell, "Are you're going nuts?! Just crazy! As if that boy wants you! If he wants you then he would be man enough to come step up and come get you're a**!"

On top of all the other things that were going on at home, I now must deal with this foolishness too. That felt like the longest night ever. Some time had passed, and we argued even more now behind it. I was even made to quit my job and was told if I didn't quit that job that I had to get out. I was more pissed now than ever. I couldn't quit that job. It was a part of my school credit. If I lose that job, I lose my credits. What am I'm going to do? Either they didn't understand, or just didn't care; but I better not keep that job. I found another job. Not that it got any better, because not long after being there, I ended up with a curfew. I was working at Burger King at the time. The dining area close at 11p.m. So after the dining area closed, I had to break the cash register down. I would have to make sure that the lobby was clean, lock the doors etc. How was I going to have an 11 p.m. curfew and still get my job done? I couldn't work no other hours because of school, and I needed all the hours I could get because of my credits. My mom always called a cab for me to get home for 11 p.m. every night. Don't know what she had heard or was hearing, but one night she decided that she was going to call the cab for me; and when the cab showed up, the driver was pissed because I wasn't ready. She called my job and told me that she had called a cab for you once, and why wasn't home yet? My manager told her that I was still working. I told my manager that she's going to call the cab again and if I'm not home in 10 minutes, I was going to be put out the house.

Instead of pulling me to the side or calling me in the office my manager decides to blurt that mess out loud in front of everybody in the store. How embarrassing! I said in a hurtful voice, "I could have called when I was done." Man, I wasn't ready. I had to finish counting my drawer. I just couldn't do my job. My mom called once again with the same old thing. And here goes my manager again yelling through the store, "Your mom said that your clothes going to be outside waiting for you if you do not show up this time!" I clearly felt like I was the only one there with common sense. You think she would have tried to help me. Instead, she continued to embarrass me in front of the night crew. When the cab driver came back, he said it was his last time coming out. When I was finally done, dispatch said they were no longer going to come out for me because my mom called three times. I told them, "Well y'all should wait until I call instead of waiting for my mom to call." When I didn't show up at home at the time my mom wanted me there, she called back and told me that was it, and that she had given me my last chance and since I wasn't there all my sh*t would be packed and put to the road. I really truly believed that my stuff was thrown out. With the kind of months that I had been having, anything was possible. So of course I called my boyfriend up while he was at work.

He got off at the same time as I did and he didn't work that far away from me. So he would walk from there to come to see me. I guess the manager was feeling sympathetic for me because she let him in to come see me so that we could figure something out about where I was going to go. After sitting in the lobby for over an hour thinking time was passing, we decided to take the long walk, and it was a long walk. It's like 1 in the morning and we walked 30 minutes, which was a little over a mile to get to my house. We were freezing because it was so cold. We get near my house and I see bags and bags outside by my door and I told him I don't know what to do and I have nowhere to go. We sat on his aunt's porch and for a moment I was safe and calm. He told me that he will talk to his mom and have me come stay there until we can figure something out. I finally got up and I started walking towards the house and as I started grabbing at the bags, I realize that the bags were full of leaves. Not one of those bags had any of my clothes in it. I was like you got to be kidding me right. Apparently, they stayed up to see if I was going to show up for whatever and they heard me outside. They both came open the door and call me in and from there everything was out of control. Everyone is in the house screaming I felt so disrespected I was called all kinds of little b*tches among other names. I was just mad and angry and I'm like how you could allow this man to call me out my name I'm No H*e. No one could answer that.

I'm not doing anything to disrespect myself they were not trying to hear that they weren't trying to hear anything that I had to say I was so angry at my mom because of that I just couldn't believe she would allow that man to call me out my name like that. I was just hurt and for him to continue to open his mouth and say things to me I didn't want to have anything to do with him or hear anything else that he had to say. He kept screaming at me if that boy loves you, he will come to get you're a**. The only thing he wants is you're a** all he would do is get you pregnant then leave you like all those other girls. You a stupid lil dumb b*tch, still trying to convince me that he didn't want me and that my boyfriend already got kids out there. I knew that was not true, but yes, he did have one child and I knew all about it. I knew about the whole situation that led up to everything from his past not just from him, but I had talks with his mom. He didn't keep anything away from me, the minute we started dating he told me all about his son and even before I knew he had a child. My step dad said if you know so much about this boy and you said this boy loves you, if you call him right now would he come? I told him yes so, he dared me to call him. I suppose this was our test I dialed his number up the phone barely ranged, and he picked up. I don't believe five minutes have passed I don't know if he ran or flew or whatever he did but that knock at my front door came so fast. Now I have walked from my house to his house and it's like 10 minutes 15 minutes depending on how fast or slow you are walking, but the fact that he was there in a short while even amaze me, but it pissed them off even worse.

My step dad was so pissed he pulled out a riffle on us. Can you imagine the thoughts that are going through our heads? I'm like why you would have me call him over here for you to pull out this gun. Old rusty riffle looks like it came out of an 1800 cowboy movie. I don't play when it comes to someone pointing a gun in your face rusty or not it was wrong, and I was scared sh*tless. I hear my boyfriend saying to me out of respect for your mom I'm not going to be disrespectful and I'm not going to do anything to jeopardize our relationship, but I will take you away from here. I don't know how but somehow, we got out of there and we ended up at his house talking with his mom. His mom said it was cool for me to stay there as long as I needed. I didn't have any clothes I ended up having to call the police for them to release my clothes to me the next day. I stayed over by his house for a good two weeks before my mom talked me back into coming home. Saying that we were going to work things out. It didn't change the way I felt about the situation, but I loved my mom no matter what so of course I went back home. When I got back home the 3 of us had a conversation about my future relationship. They had the nerves to tell me that I would have to stop seeing my boyfriend. No way I said.

I explained to them how this man would walk over to school every single day when the bell ring just to see me before I got on the bus. How he was the only one that came into my life and not take advantage of me like others did in the past. Who in their right mind would walk 2 miles going and coming to meet somebody for maybe 20 seconds to say hello and get a quick hug before I get on the bus? Just so we can see each other. Somedays I would nearly miss the bus waiting. It wasn't like he could come stand on campus, so he had to time his arrival perfect. The fact that he did that to see me for that little time told me a lot. Since I was ban from seeing him that was our only way besides me calling and talking on the pay phone at school. Then I would call collect, but he wouldn't answer and call back, he knew it was me. In between any classes I would call him or either I will have to sneak across the road to call him at the pay phone by the local convenience store. I couldn't deal with all the things at home and they never got better it was more like things doubled or tripled I just couldn't take it anymore. I finally gave up fighting them and moved back in with my boyfriend and his family. Once I was settled there, I never looked back.

There were some incidents that happened that mom so called husband was afraid I was going to tell so he either needed me to stay or I couldn't go back at all. I found peep hole in my room and from my room to the bathroom not only that my floor was cut to get in my room from underground. Some nights when I thought someone would be standing over me in the dark and I would tell my mom they think I'm f*cking nuts. Well I set that mofo up one night and yelled mom came in he had every story in the world to why he was in my room in the dark. I know he had been watching me, but a lot of sh*t happen that couldn't be explain. I was glad to be gone from there. At the time I felt like my boyfriend became my superhero. I never had anybody in my life that was down for me and just for me willing to do anything and everything he needed to do respectfully to be with me. I was 18 and he was 19 years old when we started our lives together. We started house hunting and he had got custody of his son. Things were looking up for a change. My boyfriend was now my fiancé and he had found another job. I on the other hand started back working at the job they made me quit and continued to work at this job I had. We had big plans to save money for a house while starting our family. At the age of 20 I became pregnant with our first son it was a blessing.

HYPOCRITICAL STATEMENTS

I was told most of my life that I wasn't going to finish anything yet alone graduate high school. From the beginning I was reminded how my family didn't go to school yet graduate high school. My mom dad told me he only went to the first grade and was put in the field to work making 50 cents a week. My mom neither my dad finished high school, but I know back then they said times was hard. That they had to work to take care of their families. My mom never worked a day in her life because of her sight. It wasn't to many people I knew in my family or friends of the family that accomplished anything yet tell me I won't be worth sh*t. When they tell me I'm not going to finish something I'm like I want to prove them wrong and I got to push myself just, so they can see I'm not the person that say I am. I learned a long time ago when I was in the 6th grade that they told me I wasn't going to amount to anything, and I made that background stage for Romeo and Juliet and did reports that I was capable of making an A. When I started making those A's, I knew right then that I can do better I see myself doing better and I begin trying to push myself to the limit to do better. I see the great things that came out of it I was happy and those are the things that make me happy, so I push myself to improve myself. I didn't even know at that time what I was doing. I know now that I was setting myself for greater, but then I didn't even know. So, every time they would tell me that I wasn't going to amount to anything I want to strive to prove them wrong.

The whole time I have been doing good things I just didn't see it. I couldn't see beyond the hurt and the pain, but I was doing it. The fact remains that I brought my GPA up from a 1-point average to a 2-point average kept pushing and started making the honor roll. At the end of the day I graduated high school first in my family to do so. To see the look on their faces was priceless because they were shocked when I told them that I was graduating. What was hurtful they still couldn't accept it. The only person showed up to my graduation was my mom and my boyfriend. I was 19 when I graduated high school and I was 20 when I had my first child. Since everyone said I was going to drop out and have a baby first. My son was 4lb 7oz when he was born, I went into labor early, while at the St. Patrick's Day Parade I thought I was peeing on myself and there wasn't even and porta potty in sight. I walk home with my mom when I got there, they had taken up the toilet in both bathrooms, so I had to use the neighbor bathroom. I told my fiancé that something was wrong, and I wasn't feeling well his mom said for me to go to a nap and maybe I would feel better. I was awakened to wetness the bed was soaked, they rush me to the E.R. as soon as I stepped foot in the door my water broke. I hear a nurse scream for a chair, and they rush me to a room. The doctor had me nervous saying they had to fly me to a hospital in New Orleans because I was having complications.

I ended up going to Houma in the ambulance with bad contractions. When I get there, they hook me up to iv's etc. and I was just chilling waiting to have the baby and I didn't feel any pains. I see them coming running in the room with their team they immediately rushed over to me and asked if I was ok. I told them yes, they had seen on the monitor how bad my contractions were and wanted to see if I was ok. I told them I didn't feel any of the pains, they were worried that I didn't feel them how bad they were. The doctor had to come in and give me some meds in my iv about 5 minutes later I was screaming for dear life. I had my son, but he was taken to icu I only got to peak at him for a second. I asked about my baby every chance I got because I was worried. Two days later the doctor clears me to go home and I said what about my baby they told me that my baby boy had to stay because he wasn't big enough and he wasn't really breathing on his own. I didn't want to leave him, and I couldn't even see him before I left because we were under a tornado warning and one had touch down near the hospital knocking out power. I was told that no one was allowed to go to ICU because of everyone's safety I cried all the way home.

The nurse told me I can call anytime I liked so I called every hour on the hour. I couldn't go back and see him until a few days later. It was the hardest thing to do seeing my baby with all those tubes and wires hooked up to him I could hardly see his little body. The nurse put him in my arms I was so scared to hold him I had to give him back. My child literally could fit in the palm of my hands he was so small. I just sat there until it was time to go home. About a week later I was able to go visit to see if he was able to come home, they say he was doing better, and they wanted me to be there to feed him. He had to be 5lbs to go home and he didn't want to take his bottles. The first night was a struggle and they said I had to spend another night. During the night those machines kept going off and I was a nervous wreck. But the day came where my son and I was able to start our journey home together. At 18 I had already taken on responsibilities for another child and now one of my own. I promise to be and do better and no matter what make sure they get everything they deserved. My mom was happy for me, but my step dad wasn't so much. He told me he didn't even want me coming around my mom house. For the first few months of my pregnancy I didn't even talk to my mom much didn't even see her. I was mad at her because she let this man tell her I couldn't come over. I took it upon myself to go over while he was at work, mom had cooked, and we sat and talked even had a few laughs. When it was time for him to get off, she told me that I had to leave.

I was heartbroken behind it, so I left to keep down confusion. Over the next couple of months, I would walk over to her house and then leave before he would get off. I got tired of cutting our day short just so he wouldn't say anything. Enough was enough I told her I wasn't leaving and when he came in, he walks right passed me. I was waiting for him to say something so I can go the f*ck off, but he didn't so I continue going. Before it was don't come over here and we don't want nothing to do with your baby. When my baby came after his time in the hospital, they ended up keeping him while I worked and spoiled him. It's not right for people to come at you telling you what you can't do and they not trying to do anything for themselves. All that negative that got to me and cause me to drink and smoke. The positive thing was my baby and when the doctor said no smoking no drinking, I gave it up.

CHAPTER 9

9

VICTIM OF HIT AND RUN

Months later after having my son, and 2 days before Christmas, and I found myself in the hospital. I got myself together to go to a Christmas party for my job. It was early, so my coworker and sister-in-law at the time decided to take a slow ride on our bikes to go shopping just to pass a little time. We had dropped off our gifts and took our bikes across the bayou and we ended up at Wal-Mart. Now we didn't buy much. Just a few knick-knacks and I had picked up a special gift for my fiancé. The few things I had was in one bag and I hung it on my handle bars. Like I said, we were riding our bikes and we left to go behind Wal-Mart and go up Jackson Street because we wanted to go check some things out at another store before heading back to the party. We were making good time. We had made it in front of NAPA on Saint Patrick Highway, and I noticed a white car coming across Jackson over the bridge just speeding and losing control. I remember asking my sister-n-law, "Do you see that car up there speeding?"

She said "yeah." I told her that I was glad we were riding in the lot away from the road because that was crazy. That car wasn't even near us, then and before you know it, BAM!! All I remember seeing was black and white. I'm assuming I blacked out for a moment because I don't even remember getting hit by the car. I was nowhere near the road. I was in the NAPA parking lot nearly in the area where the customers park their cars. The parking lot don't sit that close to the road. If anyone is familiar with the area here where I live, they would know. Both NAPA and the back end of Wal-Mart are about 2 minutes away via a car; or bike, like 0.3 miles apart from each other. When that driver hit me, I was in the ditch behind that Wal-Mart. The last thing I remember before I found myself in that ditch was seeing that car on that bridge, and in a matter of seconds it hit me. You would think the guy that hit me stopped when he realized what happened, or at least to see what or whom he hit. He stopped all right, but he didn't stop close. When he stopped, he got out of his car and stood there. I was alert, so I saw everything that happened. What this man did next was unreal! He stepped out of the white car, and when he saw me, he clapped. I remember my sister-n-law screaming and hollering, "oh my God! What did you do, what did you do?" To my surprise, when he realized that I was black, he clapped and kept clapping, and said "oh" with an evil laugh, then said "n*gga, hahaha!!" And then he got in his car and took off.

Could you believe this man left the scene instead of waiting on the police? He took off so fast! I yelled out, "Get his plate number so that he can be turned in!" By end of the day, the police had caught up with him and he ended up serving time in jail. Found out that he was drunk. He had multiple charges, and I believe he got 20 plus years in prison. Thanks to a Good Samaritan who saw what happened and took off behind him. The driver had made it home and the police officers were called to his residence. I was told who the Good Samaritan was by his last name. I have yet to find him and thank him for what he did for me.

BROKEN BODY

They say I was truly blessed to be alive, and fortunate to have landed in the ditch instead of the road. While in the hospital, I had a flashback of laying in that ditch. I could see my hand full of blood, and a finger hanging off. I felt wetness running from my face as people were staring and surrounding all around me. I believe my way of thinking was f***ed up because I was worried about my Girbaud jeans being ripped up, and I only had on one shoe. I was asking for them to go find my other shoe and my bag that I got from the store. Crazy of me to be worried about those things as if my life didn't matter. All I really wanted was for them to take that d*mn neck brace off my neck. I kept repeating, "Please take this thing off of me! Nothing is wrong with my neck," to the ambulance driver.

When the doctor came into the room and asked me how I was feeling and what I thought was hurting on me, I told him everything from my waist down was hurting really bad. They took me to get an x-ray. That was the most painful x-ray I'd ever had. My whole entire body was in pain from every turn I made on that table. While waiting on the results, the police came to talk to us about the guy who hit me. They said that the car he had was reported stolen by his roommate; and when he took the breathalyzer test, his blood-alcohol level was over the limit. He was being charged with a DUI, hit-and-run, reckless driving, stolen vehicle, just to name a few. Police also brings me back a bag they thought was mine, and it turned out to be a bag of trash. I guess whoever was at the scene took my bag. The police also told me how lucky I was because the bike was in pieces and they couldn't even find some of it, along with my other shoe. One of them said that it may had been in the sugar cane field across the road. The nurse comes in to talk to the doctor and I found out I had a broken nose and a broken knuckle bone in my left index finger, which was shattered. Doctor said I had to have reconstructive surgery to put my finger back in place. Everything from my waist down felt broken, but it was badly bruised. It was swollen so bad, I had to wear knee and ankle braces. One leg was as big as both legs put together.

Doctor told my family that they had to prepare me for surgery so they could take the debris out my hand. I remember going in and talking to a few people, and when I woke up my entire arm was casted up. I thought the doctor lied to me. He said my finger was broken, not my arm. They wrote me up some prescription and I went home not long after that. Christmas Eve morning, I was home with my family and his family. I was living! I couldn't walk, but the most important thing was I able to see my first-born son and the little boy who is now a part of my life. I couldn't hold either of them, nor could I hardly walk, but just to be home with them was truly a blessing. Because out of all those things that happened to me in the past, and then after all this, God kept me here for a purpose. It could have been worse. I could have lost my life, but I was back at home. I had to go to therapy to regain movement in my finger, but couldn't afford therapy for my legs. I ended up doing it on my own with the help of my fiancé once the swelling went down. If I knew after all the therapy and everything that I had to go through that God brought me this far, He had seen me through other situations as well and I just must put my faith in him.

Sometimes you get caught up in some things and you never see it coming. I definitely didn't see this happening. My fiancé lost his last job when he found out I was in that accident, so he had to find another job. They told him it was ok to come to me. He was on the road in another state when his job called him, and he was only out for two days. They didn't care what he did, nor were they even worried about what happened. They just cut him loose. It was the holiday season with 2 kids and no job. It was hard for a bit, but once I got back on my feet, my job took me back. That made me push myself harder. We were saving every dime so that we could get our own place. I even picked up another full-time job to help get us over. Some of the money we had was stolen out of our room. I knew we had a little of $2500 saved. Nobody even knew where we hid it, nor what it was packed in. Each of us put $20 to $100 in every payday and somebody had the nerve to break into our room and take it. It was late one evening and I had worked both jobs that day. Once I got off from my second job, I went over to my mom's because I wanted to see my baby. He stayed over on weekends because I always had to work both jobs. He was almost 2 years old and I would be missing my baby all day. He was my first-born child...my heart, and I hated being away from him.

A car pulled up in front of my mom's house. I was too tired to get up. I didn't even want to walk home. The person came and knocked at the door. It was my fiancé's brother. He was a truck driver and had been on the road all day. He asked me to go take a ride to New Orleans to pick up his kids from his mother-n-law. I really didn't want to go, but mom was like go because he is tired, and your company can keep him up. I had no problem going. He used to tell funny jokes, so he would keep the both of us up. By the time we got there, their kids weren't ready to go home. So, we had to wait for them to pack. Once we got home, I called my mom to tell her I had made it in. It was super late. She told me to call my cousin because she had called for me earlier that day. I wish we had cell phones back then because what happened next was mind blowing literally. Door busts open and it's another one of my fiancé's brothers. He comes in with an attitude and asked, "Did anyone call for me?" I said 'no.' At this point I am on the phone with my cousin. I began to tell her that I was going to speak to her tomorrow or call her from our house phone in our room. Call waiting...I say 'hello' to the person on the other end. They ask for another person in the home. I told them to hold on. I wasn't sure if the person was there or not. Click over to tell my cousin I will talk with her later. Click back, the person on the other end had hung up.

Man, I was so tired that I just I just slouched down on the couch. My fiancé's brother came back in and asked, 'You sure nobody called?' I had told him what just had happened, but the phone wasn't for him. He goes outside and comes back in with attitude again and said, 'I need to use the phone.' He grabbed the cordless phone and went outside. He came back in and started yelling at me, saying "I need you to learn to answer the mother f*cking phone!" I told him the phone wasn't for him and I told him nobody called for him and that I wasn't even at the house that long before he came back in. I heard him ask someone "what time?" Yelling once again, "what time?" You can hear him screaming at the person he was talking to. Well, what happens when you get caught up between two people that are playing over each other?

As we walked into the house after returning from New Orleans, he told his older brother's girlfriend that he was going out to meet this chick, but another chick was coming over to see him. He was trying to cover his a** so that he wouldn't get caught up; but things started to backfire. He was cheating on his girlfriend and his girlfriend was cheating on him. While they both were trying to get their excuses together, I get caught in the middle, I guess. I could hear him tell the girlfriend that when he walked in, he saw me on the phone. She used that as an excuse and ran with it. She said that she called, and I didn't answer the phone. Next thing I remember, he's screaming at me.

So I decided to get up so I can go to my room. When I got up, he pushes me down onto the sofa. One thing he didn't know about me was that nobody, and I mean nobody, puts their hands on me! I don't care how big you are! When my dad proceeded to beat me for no reason when he asked where my mom was, and he beat me because I didn't know, and he put that belt down and I picked it up and beat him. Who does this man think he is putting his hands on me? I got up and I swung, knocking his face to one side. I didn't think that wasn't a good idea because that was the only lick I got off him. He whipped my a** with that cordless phone in his hand and his girlfriend on the other end. I remember screaming to the top of my lungs to him saying, "Please stop, I'm not going to hit you anymore!" He said, "B**** I know you're not going to hit me! Who the f*** you think you are?" He continued to beat me, hitting me with the phone, punching and kicking me into the sofa. I watched their baby brother (who was my best friend and who I thought was like a brother to me) come out with one of his friends, walk over to the icebox, open it, turned, and watched what was happening, then walked away. I was hurt even more as I'm lying on the couch all bloodied up, and can't move because I'm in pain. I can see him walk off and put the battery pack back on the phone, and then proceed on with his conversation. My God kids' mom came running towards me and helped me get to my room. She called my fiancé at work. It was like as soon as she hung up the phone, he was there.

All I could hear was a bunch of arguments going on in the hallway. I'm lying in the room in the bed in pain, head is killing me. By this time, his brother had taken off. They took me to the police station. After about 2 or 3 minutes of being there, they looked at me and said that they had to bring me to the emergency room right away. The doctor said that my head was gashed open and I was going to have to have staples to close it up. I had around three or four extra knots on my head, knots and bruises all over my arm, and not to mention my engagement ring was crushed to my fingers and the ring had to be cut off.

I didn't have a home to go back to because I was put out due to something he did. He always seemed to do something wrong and get away with it. It is the middle of the night and we are now away from both kids. I called up my cousin, who stayed 2 blocks over, and we were able to go to her house to pass some time. It was like four in the morning, and we stayed there until like six or seven a.m., then drove around the street and snuck back into the house to get some sleep. Over the next few days, it was a lot of tension in the house; but karma, ha, it comes back! That next weekend, someone put his head through a glass. He had to get stitches from his face to the midpoint of his head. He lied about what happened, but the streets all had the same story.

A few weeks later, his girl came over and decided to talk out the side of her face. So, I confronted her and told her "don't sit there and talk about me!" I'm not a messy person. I could have told him how she had been cheating on him, and he was driving her other man's car while he was offshore, and she said it was the aunt's car. I could have told her how he was cheating, even that same night. That night, they both had plans to go out, but tried to get out of the date with each other to be with somebody else. She tells us things and so does he. All I do is shake my head saying to another member of the house that, "that s*** will catch up to them." Who would have known I would get caught in the middle?

D***, I should have ratted them out for all that. She continued to talk stupid after I called her out, so we ended up outside and we began to fight. So, I spoke up and told them both off about how they had no sympathy at all; and that they were users and selfish people. Some time had passed. He even went to jail for doing what he did. A few years later after he did that time, he comes at me with some bullsh*t a** apology by hitting on me. Telling me how sexy I am. He had no shame nor respect. It had been years since I wore a dress because of my past. I found that it was easy to access. When people saw me, they saw the tomboyish side. I wore baggy pants and a t-shirt, tennis shoes, or boots. That weekend, I went to a family wedding where another brother was getting married. We all shared a room. Despite what happened in the past, I felt as if it was behind us because we all moved on from that.

Jump past us getting through the night to the next morning, we all are getting ready because they must be at the church, my fiancé and him. His girlfriend and I had to get dressed last. Once I was done, I stepped out the bathroom and all eyes were on me, mouths dropped. The girlfriend said, "Damn girl, I didn't know you knew how to dress like that!" I started to go off, like wtf that meant. Three days later, we are back home, and my fiancé brother asked, "Can I talk to you?" I said, "Sure what's up?" That's when the bullsh*t a** apologizes came.

He never said just sorry. He said, "That time I hit you, that was my bad. Girl, you looked too good in the dress for us to be mad." That was the past. I was no longer mad. Just stayed my distance and spoke when needed. "Well, we can do better," he said. "But what kind of stocking was that you had on? Look just like your skin." He asked because he wanted to get his girl some to match hers like that. Told me how good I looked in my dress said I was fine, and don't take it the wrong way. I said, "thanks I guess," and walked out the door.

FUEL TO FIRE

I literally had to start dealing with that craziness. He started writing me love letters and giving me money; started stalking me and harassing me, and even buying me knee-high stockings. He told me he would pay me just to wear them and he wants to see me in them for just a minute. Even came knocking on my door one night and said that he was going to tell that I was cheating if I didn't sleep with him. He was so drunk one night that he came knocking at my window while my fiancé was at work, and told me I better open or he was going to call him at work and tell him I was cheating. I was like, "Do you want me to give you the phone? Better yet, I'll call him for you. Please just go away."

Neither my fiancé nor I put two and two together that he would always call him on the job and ask what time he was getting off. My fiancé worked late, and got off 2 am...sometimes 3 am on weekends because he was a store manager at a fast food place. Thing is, he didn't care. We told on him and he came to me one day and said, "Who going to stop me or whip my ass? I'm grown!" Every opportunity he had, he tried to get at me. He sent me pictures of his private so many times, texted me love notes. I changed my number and everything. He found a way to get at me. Even when the family was around, he would walk around and show people pictures in his phone. When he gets to me, it's a d*** pic of him.

He even came to my house and stole my pictures off the wall, and nobody in the house even realized it was gone...until he asked to borrow a magazine and returned it directly to me followed by these words: "Look inside before you put it down." My picture and a letter. No matter what we did, he would not stop sending me letters and offering me whatever change he had in his pocket. I became terrified, I even had a dream that seemed so real, that one night he came to my house and somehow drugged me carried me out took me to his house in his room and raped me. I was just lying there helpless, and his face was blurry. When I came through, I was fighting him off me and kicking him. I ran for the door, but couldn't get out. I saw the window open kicked out the screen, jumped out, and ran home crying. I made it to my sofa. He followed me and started banging at my door screaming, "I want you and I need you! My brother is no good for you! I hear boom, boom, boom. Yet again, boom, boom, boom. I jump up. I was dreaming and before I fell asleep, I had been cutting the grass out in the yard and cleaned up my house, cooked, and took my shower. I had grabbed me some milk and cookies, turned on the TV, and fell asleep on the sofa. Once awakened by the booming noise, which was a knock on the door, I had to collect my thoughts. I asked, "Who is it?" It was my fiancé other brother's wife. She asked me if I was ok.

It seemed so real and my glass of milk was almost empty. I didn't remember drinking that much, but I guess I did. I just poured the rest out because I was afraid to drink it. I went next door and had a conversation with my soon to be sister-in-law and I told her about the dream, and how it felt so real. This crap went on for years. We concluded that something was wrong, and he needed help. After a while, I didn't let him worry me. Just ignored the fact that he came at me that way. I mean you must be some type of sick person to feel some type of way for your brother's girl.

I even stayed clear of his girlfriends, trying not to get close to them because he would still try to talk to me while in their presence, blow me kisses, etc. My fiancé claimed to talk to him every time I tell him, or when I gave him the money that he would give me. It stops for a while, then starts again. And threatening him didn't work, nor going to jail. It doesn't faze him. One of his girlfriends found a letter. Well, sort of a letter. She found a notebook under the mattress and took a pencil and rubbed over it, and read the info on it. I felt bad for her because I never told her he was doing this to me. But people can act. He was good at hiding, cheating, and lying. She was the only one left in the dark. She asked everyone if they knew about it. We all told the truth. She was hurt and wanted to fight me. I then sat and told her everything. She eventually left him.

I stayed clear of the girlfriends because some people would get mad at you, or think you lying and really want their man. I had no time for it. I had a friend of mine back in school break off our friendship because I knew her boyfriend hugged another girl, whom happened to come to visit the school. The girl was his cousin, who had graduated and came back to visit after she went off to college, and he gave her a hug. I was wrong for not saying anything, I saw no big deal. If it was another girl, maybe. There were dozens of others I stayed clear of; at least I tried. I am a nice person, so I bond with people and made friends with a few. Today they know the truth, and we are still cool. I was concerned about me because no matter how many girls he had, he told me how bad he wanted me and one day he was going to get me. Never let your guard down, because when you do, you have been caught slipping.

That's just what happened to me. I got caught slipping. The letters stopped and so did the calls. Like I said, I changed my number a few times. One day he called asking to borrow some flour. I told him I didn't think I had any, wanting to say no. But he came over. Kids were all gone. My fiancé, who was now my husband, at that time, I hadn't seen him in days; and I was home alone. For years, he been telling me how he was going to get me. He finally caught me that day. He said he came to show me something on his phone. He even said, "It's not what you think." Because he knew I wasn't going to look if it was another picture of his private.

I'm halfway in my house at the door with one foot on the porch step. It is big bright daylight. I couldn't see what he was showing me because the sun is hitting my front porch. He was like, "Step back a bit." I'm like, "I can't see it. Let me see the phone so I can get back to what I was doing." I backed in my house just a bit, I never seen what was on the phone. At that point on that day, he snatches me up! He picked me up, took me to my sofa, and pinned me down. The way he grabbed me, I ended up on the sofa with one arm behind my back and he had my other arm pinned with his hands and my legs with his. His free arm was pulling my pants off and undoing his, and he starts to have his way with me. Kissing me and performing oral sex. Telling me how bad he wanted me. How long he wanted me and how good I tasted. Reaching up feeling on my breast. He pulled my bra up to my neck and played with my nipple with his tongue. He goes back down on me and play with me with his fingers. Before he could manage to penetrate me fully, I was able to break away my arm; and I kicked and kicked, screaming, telling him I was going to call the police; and told that him if he didn't get off, he was going to jail for life, and it was his third strike!

He said, "Let me just have this one time and I promise to leave you alone. Nobody could hear you scream, everyone is gone." What I felt down there was either 3 maybe 4 inches of him trying to penetrate my insides and him repeating "F***" over and over. He was mad because it wouldn't get hard. I was on pins and needles, scared sh**less of what he might do next. He finally was taking what he wanted and couldn't fully get it, while I'm still screaming. My house sat in the back. All the neighbors around me worked, but the houses weren't close like that. My house sat in the center of surrounding streets, so all other houses sat facing the road while I was like the center of everyone's backyard surrounded by a fence from all neighbors. He did his homework and found the right time to make his move. After all the screaming, he snaps at me. I turned my head. He misses as he tries to slap me. He's still saying crap. I'm trying not to cry, trying to focus on getting him off me. He takes another lick of my private spot and head to my nipples, sucking and biting. He tried to penetrate again, I can feel him on me, but he still can't get it up.

He said, "Come for me, please." I don't know where my strength came from. I made him drop by kicking him in between his legs, yelling "Please get out! I won't report you if you stop now." Reiterating what I told him before. Screaming and yelling "please, please get out." I told him, "Think of your kid. You need to stop this. If I send you to jail again, you won't see him. He promised me that he wasn't going to come at me again. I ran and locked the door. So ashamed, mad, and hurt I took a shower and waited on my kids. I was alone with no one to talk to. When my husband came back, it was nothing to say about it. I was too busy arguing with him about his whereabouts over the last few days; and on top of it all, he was drunk. For so long, I didn't even blame my attacker. I blamed him. Even after I told him about what happened, he didn't even get mad. Didn't say much on it. That had me in a rage. Mentally I was going nuts. How can this man not express anything? I have now been robbed, knocked out, stalked, had my head busted open, and nearly raped...on top of everything else. I have every reason to be mad and angry; and now you see why I'v been BROKEN. What was this thing called life to me? My life didn't feel like my own. Everyone wanted a piece of me in some way. All my husband wanted was a wife who had his back no matter what, because he knew I would be there. And he was all I knew.

CHAPTER 10

10

ONCE A CHEATER

Like any typical relationship, we had our ups and downs. But as the kids got older, I found myself asking about time being spent with them. He could always find time to spend with his homeboys, but not his boys. That became a problem for me. I felt some type of way whenever the homeboys would come over with their kids. Just couldn't understand how you can go hang out with others and theirs, but not you and yours Our son was in Head Start and I was called over to the school one day for some reason, I don't remember. But I do remember being over at the school and my phone rang, and it was him. The way he responded didn't sound right. After I said hello, it was like I had this weird feeling came over me, and he said, "We need to talk." Before I could let him say anything else, I don't know why, but the first thing that came out of my mouth was, "Are you leaving me?"

There was silence on the other end of the phone. I decided to stay on the outside of the classroom because, at that moment, my whole world felt like it was crashing right in front of me. I had quickly snapped back to reality, headed back to the class, grabbed my things, and walked home. I did not understand, I was having flashbacks trying to remember when and what went wrong. I came up with nothing but me asking him to spend time with his kids. And we didn't argue that much. I didn't know what was going on. When I got home, I called him, and he wouldn't answer the phone at first. The water works began. I was nervous and shaking. After a few tries, I got him to answer. I started asking questions like, "Who you cheating on me with?" Like, "What is going on and why, why you leaving me?" For this man to tell me that he was leaving all because I pissed him off by asking him to spend time with his kids, I said, "You must be f*cking kidding me!" What kind of man would leave his woman because she fussed behind taking care of what supposed to be yours? We have a family. We have a home. You going to break up over this nonsense? I called him all kinds of names. I told him that he wasn't a real man, and only boys would do something like that; and he was more of a man when he was a boy than what he was being right at that moment. The person I am today never would have pulled what I did back then. I wasn't in my right mind at times. Had all types of evil thoughts going through my head.

I knew he couldn't resist having sex with me, so I set him up. But of course I wasn't no dummy! I had my own protection when he came over. I put on this lotion with the glitter in it and lipstick that comes off, but clear enough to where he didn't notice. I figured I had to outsmart him on this one, so that when he went back to her, every bit of me would be on him. Only to be recognized by her eyes and he caught on later, but still not enough that she wouldn't notice. I was in love with this man, so who would have known months later I would take him back after all the stuff that the other girl put us through. Even years down the road, she still comes back to haunt us. After he found out what she really was about, he ended up leaving her alone. I just think at the time, we both were so young being together and we never both thought about things that could affect our relationship. We both took on building a family and a home, so I guess it scared him. It scared me too, but we ended up working it out. The both of us ended up getting new jobs. This girl would call the job and start stalking us, lying saying all kinds of things; until finally we had to get a restraining order on her. Although I told him I had forgiven him and had taken him back, I never truly forgave him because the sh*t hurt, and it caused a lot of hurt in our family. I lied because I wanted him back no matter what. The day I had to tell our first born we had together that their dad wasn't no longer living with us was hard. He was a smart kid and you couldn't keep nothing from him.

To see my child in the kitchen by the sink sitting with his knees in front his face, and not moving or saying a word messed me up inside. He sat there for hours not talking to anyone. I shed more tears and I just had to get his dad back. I was willing to lie to get him back, even if it was for our kids to be seen by him. Every time something happened, although we thought we were rid of her, something else comes back that she had done that would affect our lives again. The woman I was then didn't let that sh*t go. Our relationship was in jeopardy because of it, all because of the stupid thing that he wanted to do instead of sitting down as a man to have a conversation with his woman. He thought he could go find it elsewhere. He would find out that the grass wasn't greener. This girl somehow got our numbers. I don't know how. She would call my phone cussing me out. Now he would find out how a few weeks of pleasure can cause a lifetime of pain. Even when he was messing around with her when he would be at work, she found a way to get at me to say things or to do things. It only got worse when they were no longer together. 10 weeks had nothing on the years the pain that she would bring to our family and what he brought to our family. Finally, after a while she stops; but then she started up again this time through the courts, sending a court order with the documents saying that her child was his. Now we had already been through this once with a paternity test, but she wasn't taking no for an answer. She truly wanted her baby to be his, so she moved to another state and had another test done.

I guess she didn't get it the first time when it said 99.9 percent that the baby wasn't his. After the second time, we didn't hear anything again for a while. This would have me walking around pissed off, especially the first time because if that kid was his, I knew for a fact it was going to be a living nightmare. Although we weren't married yet, I loved this man and wanted it to work. Things got better for a while, and we had our second child together. But it wasn't long before sh*t would hit the fan. The same day out the hospital, I would find myself alone with a baby and pain. This man dropped me off at home, went out to get my meds, and never came back. I was hurt even more. My heart couldn't take anymore pain. How low can a person get? I found myself sinking deep into postpartum depression, and the fear of being alone had set in. I couldn't eat, and at one point I couldn't sleep. I stayed away from people and wouldn't answer any calls. I just felt hopeless, but that small child would cry. And no matter what state of mind I was in, my baby would pull me out...which made my bond even stronger with him. So my kids became my #1. Again, I forgave and moved on. As we both worked, I had other plans for my life such as going back to school and to continue working with the youths. As I started making more money, things got worse. He wanted to be the breadwinner.

I told him to get another job if it was going to be a problem that I was making more money than he was. I didn't see the big deal because what was mines was all ours. Long as those bills were paid and we had what we needed, it didn't matter to me. What I would never understand is why a man can't talk to you about their problems? They would rather keep things locked in. That was his problem. I had been with this man since we were kids, and 3 kids down the road, and all the ups and downs. I can tell what wasn't right with him. He wouldn't admit it to me. Unlike other things, I would find out about him over the years. Looked like the more I tried, the further we grew apart. I felt as if we needed a break and one day I just had enough. I had fallen out of love with the man I thought was my everything. I finally left but I wanted to work it out, so I left long enough for him to realize what he had and what he could lose. I know I am not perfect, but I was damn good to him. All I mainly wanted was partly for him to spend time with his boys alone, then it became time with just the two of us. Instead, the streets had him. The late hours of coming in were killing me and he would sleep all day, get up to go to work, and stay out until 2 or 3 am. I just couldn't. It didn't take long for him to come to his senses and realize it. A lot had to be said to each other and get out what the problem was before we could get back to us again.

Child number 3 comes along, number 4 for him. Now don't get me wrong, we had more good times than bad. It was just that the bad was starting to overpower the good. The stealing my debit card, lying, having no money to pay our bills. We kept getting our lights and water cut off, but I always found a way to get it back on. Some loans here and there. Before we knew it, we were in so much debt. As the saying goes, we were robbing Peter to pay Paul. Sh*t, we robbed Peter and paid Paul, then turned around and robbed Paul a** to pay someone else or just to eat. I had to start paying attention to little things. He became too friendly and always wanted to go by one of our friend's house. She always needed something fixed. At first, I wasn't tripping because I didn't think she would do anything to hurt me, and he told me that he only love people his own skin color. Always reminded me to keep my body a certain size. I had gotten a little overweighed. Went from 110 to 170, but our friend was well over 250. I used to get mad when he would talk about her and I would be like, "That is your friend, how can you talk about her?" He said, "That's your friend and I don't care...that's nasty!"

I met her through him. They used to work together. She was one of the coolest white girls I knew since school. I didn't see her as a white girl. I just saw her, but she liked black guys she had a little girl by this deadbeat...as she called him, and we could sit down and just talk about our problems. Big mistake! That was a lesson learned on my part. Over some years we had been shopping, hanging at each other houses, sleeping over after parties. I even invited her to my family's house during the hurricanes. We both had been through a lot, but I never would have thought that she would be sleeping with my husband. When did they even find the time? I started putting two and two together to figure out what was going on. After work, I would be exhausted, so they knew I would fall asleep and I would fall asleep anywhere. She always wanted to be outside with him. They both smoked, so I would stay in. Any excuse they had they used. I was locked up in my room one day when someone very close to me came in and said they needed to talk to me, but didn't know where to start and said you heard it from me. The news was shocking. I couldn't believe it. They say a drunk person tells the truth when they are drinking, but to confess that info to that person was evil in my book. I felt like he wanted me to know. I was all kinds of f*cked up behind this. I caught a ride because we only had one car. Besides, he was glad I didn't drive, meaning I couldn't spy on him. Little did he know I had my ways of getting around.

After all the months had gone by, I had my suspicions, but couldn't really confirm them. One thing about me, I used to let people take advantage of me, but I never would forget. I remember certain things that were said in codes and locked it in until I need them because payback will come, and everyone will pay for what they did to me. I arrived at my so-called friend's job and sat thinking of a plan and how I will go to her. I wanted to beat the sh*t out of her. I thought about me going to jail and my kids and her daughter. That's what saved her. I walked in, but she wasn't there. I had asked the girl behind the counter for her and she said she was going to get something from the back of the store, so I waited. When she saw me, she was like, "Heyyy girl, what are you doing here, shopping?" In my head, I'm like B*TCH NO, here to beat you're a**! Then I felt bad because I don't believe in calling people B*tches like that. I smiled and said we need to talk. She came around and I asked her, what the f*ck was going on with her and my husband. She was like, "What you mean?" I said, "Y'all sleeping together." Damn, silence cuts deep! What do you know? I had to turn around and look behind. S*** you would have thought someone was behind me from the look on her face. I said, "You saw a ghost, cause you look shocked. I don't want any trouble." She said, "I don't want any motherf*cking trouble either, just the truth. All the sh*t we have been through and you sleeping with my n*gga behind my back?" She said, "No, it's not like that." I was like, "Well wtf it's like because I'm 2 seconds on you're a** girl."

She said, "A few years ago, when I first started working with him, you two were on bad terms and we, well, I just did oral sex on him, but that was it, I promise." Now the woman I am, I never would've went to another woman's house knowing I have been with her man in any kind of way. Some people have no respect. I wanted the truth. All of it. She said, "It was a few times, but that was all that happened." I left her job, so she could get back to work. I waited for her to get off so we could talk. That's all I wanted. I went to her house, she wouldn't even open the door for ne; said she was going to call the police. I just wanted to know if my man was there because he was gone for 3 days; and the last I heard, they were together. I left though. I was all kinds of stupid because this man was back home by nightfall and all he could say was he was out with the guys. He convinced me that she was crazy and had lied on him. They never had relations and she wanted to, but he said no. I called bullsh*t. I told her if I ever saw her near him even call him, I wasn't going to be so nice next time. I even told him to lose her number, we are no longer friends. And we had a good friendship, so I thought. She apologized for what she did, but it wasn't good enough for me. I never trusted my husband again. I never talked with her again until months down the road.

I paid someone to follow my husband and take pictures just to see if he was out there doing something...and he was. I would give him the benefit of the doubt and give him a chance to own up to some of his sh*t. He told lie after lie. I even told him I had pictures. He laughed in my face. I even seen him with my own eyes. That much he knows is the truth. I made him bring his a** home that night I caught him. He promised he was done then, but the lies caught up.

CHAPTER 11

11

BROKEN FAMILY

When I experienced my first heartbreak with a guy I loved, I was in high school. I thought I was in love, but the way my life was set up the relationship wasn't working as I wanted it to. I guess my boyfriend at that time wasn't understanding the fact that the only time that we got to spend time together was at school at lunch and breaks in between classes. Weren't many phone calls. I had to sneak and use the phone, and every time we will have a chance for him to come over, they would give him the third degree. Asking all those questions like, "Who he is related to?" Then when he leaves say, "Y'all related." This guy, I was down for him. My girlfriend told me that she saw him writing love letters to his ex-girlfriend. I didn't want to believe it. I even asked him about it, but of course he denied it; so I gave him the benefit of the doubt and I believed him. Mardi Gras was coming up and before that day came, I went to talk to my mom and stepdad about him coming over. But she had some rules, so course I'm excited. I go to school and share the news with him and he's like "okay."

We made plans for that day and I couldn't wait because finally, my mom was allowing me to do something. That morning, I remember sitting on the front steps. I waited for him to come and he never showed up. I was hurt a little bit, but I made all kinds of excuses up in my head. Like maybe he went with family or whatever, that's why he didn't come. Maybe his mom said no. I didn't know, so I went on and tried to enjoy my day. My aunt lives two blocks over, so we walked to her house to go catch the parade on the other end. I really I didn't want to be engaged in a conversation with anyone, so I went and sat on her front porch watching the crowd passing by. But what do you know. I see two people walking hand-in-hand and one of them happened to be my boyfriend. I tell you when he saw me, it was like he had seen a ghost. He jumped back, and he let her hand go so fast. The rest of my day was ruined. The morning of our return at school when I saw him, he tried to give me every excuse in the book to why he was walking with her and why he was holding her hand, while trying to calm me down. I wasn't trying to hear any of that. We kind of got into a heated argument down the hall and I told him that I hated him. I slapped him in the face and walked away.

He began to shed a tear and started begging me to stay. I was too hurt. Even more so because I had got my mom and stepdad to let me have a boyfriend. They talked about everyone I knew, trying to keep me away from any guy. When I was no longer talking about him, the attitude stopped. The pain that I experienced from that was nothing but hurt. I was hurt for days, weeks. Eventually, I got over it, but that pain was nothing like the pain I would experience years later. Having your heart broken is one thing, but to have your heart broken, stomped on, chewed and spit out...that's another thing. The saying is true when they say that people will come in your life for a reason. Some people come in your life for a season and some for a lifetime. Some people are there to show you a path and hopefully, you can grow from within that pathway, but nothing that you would ever do will help you grow if you don't know how to overcome it. See, that was my problem...overcoming. I didn't know how to overcome, but I knew how to sink deeper into my depression. The smartest thing I did was keep a journal of our talks just so I could catch him in his lies just in case I needed it someday. I can't keep sitting back and play the fool. Many times, he claims to have been robbed. Now the first time maybe you would believe it; but after 3 or 4 times, it starts to become a pattern. Now I had fallen out of love with this man before and fallen back in love with him over the course of years.

So many things happened. We had ups and downs, but I knew I loved this man and I wanted to make it work, only because we had kids and I know what I've been through in the past coming from a broken home. I didn't want my kids to become a part of that, so I did whatever was necessary to do so my kids can have their family. I'm thinking this is the best thing for all of us, although they rarely saw him there. Anytime he would be home, he would spend with them, even if it was 10 minutes or 30 minutes. I felt that was better than none. I do know whenever he wouldn't come home at times, they would ask for him. I did everything in my power that I could possibly think of to try to keep us together. There times that we were happy. I just miss the days when we used to take family trips and it didn't really cost us anything. We would just leave...pack up on a Thursday, skip out on school on Friday, and come back Sunday and be ready for school on Monday morning. I often miss those times. Somewhere we failed in our relationship and it was just me and the kids. When we got married, everything was great at first. But somehow it just wasn't working for me. I figured if we got married that things might change. He would have to stay home but that wasn't the case. It seemed as if the more I tried, the more he pulled away. I became more and more depressed, started gaining weight, and I cried my eyes out. Plenty of nights I cried myself to sleep and I tried to hide it from the kids.

The older kids knew that something was wrong. Crazy thing is the oldest kids came to me and said that I should leave their dad. They even told me that they believe he's out there doing something, and I don't deserve to be treated the way he was treating me. It was because of them I wanted to stay. He was my husband and their father, and I wanted to do anything to work it out. I used to walk the streets in the middle of the night looking for this man. I was out in the streets 1, 2, 4 in the morning. Sometimes I would walk the neighborhood for hours, even go to places where I believe he would be at. A lot of times I wouldn't find him, but this man was like a magician. When I'm out searching for him and I get home after all the time walking and looking, suddenly, he would pop up from out of nowhere and I would ask him, where the hell he been. "I was just around the corner," he said. I just left that corner and you wasn't on it. Stop lying to me! There were plenty of nights that I walked the streets and it's freezing out. It's so cold, I could barely feel my hands. Whenever I would find him and we get back home, all we would do is argue, and then I would be mad with him and we would stay in separate rooms. I just wanted him home. I didn't even care if he was in the other room. There were days that I let things go under. Only thing I ever worried about was making sure the kids ate, bathed, and got their school work done. Nothing else mattered. I felt like I didn't matter. I thought that he didn't love me and he just didn't care, and no matter how hard I tried, nothing seemed to be working. Even after all of this, I would still go out in the streets and look for this man…until one night, something happened.

Now you might think I'm crazy, but I was out about 4 blocks away from home when I realized it. I was like, forget it. I'm just going back home. I was almost a block and a half away from the house and I hear a strange noise. The strange sound was a vehicle. I knew it was, but something was not right about it. It was almost like something was coming for me, and the closer it got, I started jogging. It got closer, and every time it would hit a side street, I will hear the sound of the engine. Now no one else is outside that could see. It's about 3 a.m. and the horn sounded like something from a horror movie. As it got closer, I start running faster, and I ran, and I ran, and I ran. As I made it into my yard, it seemed as if it was right there and I went into the house, locked my door, and headed into the room. I ended up going in the next bedroom, cutting out the lights, and peeking out the window to see if I could see anything. I never did. I let it go. I never went back out there again. That night taught me a hard lesson. I was never scared of walking the streets and I had seen things beyond my beliefs. I don't know Who, What, or Why, but I know this: I would never put myself in a place that could cause me my life. I was in fear for the first and last time. Meanwhile, time just passed and as it passed, and I just stopped caring. I said I was going to stick it out until my oldest, biological child makes 18, but that was the time I allowed for him to change and hopefully he could see that.

Instead, I tried to focus on myself. I went back to school and did for my kids. Things started getting harder and harder. Looked like every time I tried to make a step forward, I got knocked a step and a half back. It felt more like I got thrown back a thousand steps. I blame myself for a lot of things because I am thinking, what I did wrong and how can I fix it. That was my problem. I tried to fix everything, even if I knew it wasn't going to work. I knew I was covered by God because plenty of times when we didn't have,

I would cry my eyes out and the next day it would be there. I was crying because our lights were about to get cut off and somehow I ended up with the money. I was crying because we didn't have any food, and somehow, we ended up with groceries. Only thing that kept me calm was my crafting. So I would lock myself in my shop and I would work until I got tired. Doing my crafts saved me plenty of times because whenever my husband somehow lost his check or go blow his check, I was able to sell my craftwork and we would get by off that money. I would sometimes do craft shows and that helped, but we all know that it takes money to make money; so I had to think outside of the box. I knew I didn't have much money to spend on supplies, so I started finding other things that I could make and put together to sale. I started watching a lot of YouTube videos learning how to make things from things we already had, things people had thrown away and doing upholstery.

I became really good at it. I started finding new ways to make new items and change others up to something more updated. It became my life every chance I had when I wasn't busy dealing with our kids. While crafting gave me something to look forward to, my husband tried to take it from me. We got into an argument one day and he told me that all I wanted to do was sit in my shop and make that bullsh*t. He didn't even realize that what ie was doing caused us to be in a lot of holes that I dug us out with the money from that bullsh*t. That was over the top. It hurt me to my heart because now I felt like it was something else being taken away from me. He asked me to quit one of my jobs while working two jobs to spend more time at home. I finally do that. Then when I'm not working, we get into an argument. Then he's saying that I need to find a job. I go in fussing saying that he needed a better job with benefits. How can you want me to be a stay-at-home mom with nothing? How we are supposed to raise our kids this way? You want to talk about bullsh*t? That's some bullsh*t. This bullsh*t may I add, tides us over when you f*ck up and we made it through another day, another week, even another month, sometimes off of that bullsh*t.

I didn't want to hear anything else that he had to say. I ignored him for weeks. I was hurt! My anxiety kicked in, then I started having health problems. I didn't know what was going on with my body. I went to the doctor and they ran several tests. They told me everything is good, but I didn't feel good. While walking home from the emergency room one day, I remember calling my sis and I was talking to her about it because she was studying to be a doctor. I told her about my symptoms that I was having and I told her that they didn't find anything wrong with me. But she also knew majority of the things I was going through and she told me that it was most likely stress. She told me some things that I could do to de-stress myself. Surely it was stress. was only relieved a little bit, but it was so many things happening repeatedly, it just became too overwhelming. Things that thought I could handle I no longer could handle, so I started drinking again. I had another job and whenever I would get off from work, I would go to the store. Every day I would do this and buy a 40. After I got home and drink my beer, I would go take a relaxing bath, feed my kids, get them straight, and lock myself in my room. Nobody knew what was going on with me. I would go off to work or community, and just be me as if nothing was happening. Nothing was bothering me...always smiling. I only talked to who I needed or wanted, but somewhere deep down in me I knew I was wrong. I felt like a hypocrite because, how can I be out letting others know what not to be doing, but I am allowing this to happen in my own home?

It was just sad, but I continued to drown my sorrows in my 40 and sleep until eventually things got worse. Nothing is no longer working. I burst out. I couldn't concentrate on school and my grades started suffering, but I didn't give up that quick. I finished the semester out and when it was time to reapply, I just didn't. I couldn't because I couldn't grasp everything that was going on. I was having problems with my stepson, dealing with counseling, outbursts, and disrespect; but it wasn't always. Just bad sometimes. We had some good days in between that, but then he wanted to hang in the streets and I confronted him and I also told his dad about it. But instead of dad putting his foot down and backing me, behind my back he was telling them it's okay because they were boys. Seemed as if the only time he would get mad was when the kids did something he didn't like. When they did wrong, I was told I didn't know how to fuss and tell him to get on them. He would tell me, "well they got to learn; how else they going to learn from their own mistakes." Learning from mistakes is one thing, but how about manning up and putting your foot down when you need to? I was no way cool with that at all. I got angry! And the angrier I got, the worst things got. I was mad all the time. I had to fight a battle within myself. I know I couldn't stay in my depression too long, but it wasn't anything I could turn on and off. I knew I had to beat it somehow, especially when you thought about self-harm.

I stopped talking to my husband because he would no longer answer me about seeking help. I became resentful and he had nothing to say to me unless it was about the kids, and that was the only thing we talked about. I had so much hatred towards this man. Whenever he would be home, I would ask him if he had anywhere he needed to be because I could no longer stand him or even want him in the same house sharing the same space with me. It was just a side of him that made me sick, not to mention the days he would be gone weekends at a time and the smell from the alcohol and being in the same clothes for days drove me nuts. This time I really let myself go. I started staying home in my night clothes and had no care in the world. I was just numb. Everyday things had gotten so bad that I had to put one child out and another child said that he no longer wanted to be there.

TORN

That whole time I was fighting for my husband and trying to keep my family together, but the more I tried, the more things fell apart. "I'm staying because of the kids" is what I kept telling myself, but I didn't even see that they were suffering just as much as I was. I thought I was protecting them from seeing and knowing, but that was making it worse. It's bad when your child even comes back and tell you what their friends have seen and said. Now I am the mom that's lying to her kids and they feel like they can't trust what I am telling them.

Now I didn't want to put my son out, but out of anger I told him he needed to get his sh*t and leave if he thought he was grown, because I didn't want him out in the street doing things that he shouldn't be doing, and it really upset me. At the same ime, I wanted his dad to step in. I wanted his dad to put his foot down finally and tell him, today is the day that you stop. It didn't turn out that way. I'm saying to myself, "that's the same child that I fought for when he was a baby. Love him like my own child and here, we are now arguing and he's out in the streets calling me out my name and pulling his shirt off talking about kicking my a**!" My husband steps out and tells me to get in the house and let him be, like it was cool to be called a b*tch by your own child. When we both stepped in, I asked him why he didn't go talk to his son instead of yelling at me. I'm at the point to where we were now allowing him to smoke, sell, and just do whatever the hell he wanted. It just wasn't right, and I didn't know who this man has become. It was too much hurting going on, but when my oldest came to me and said that he no longer could take the animosity going on in the home, no one speaking to each other, his parents fussing all the time, it started affecting him and he packed up and moved out.

I was crushed! I felt like I was losing my child, even though he was going right around the corner. That just done something to me. When I tell you actions stand out, they really do. Our actions caused all the problems. And then there was three. It was now just the three of us; myself and my two youngest. Oh, but my husband was still living there. He just was never home. My baby boy was too young to understand what was going on, but our second child together, it really started affecting him. He started asking questions about his brothers' whereabouts, where's Dad. And I'm the type of person to keep it real, so I would never hide anything anymore from my kids, so I told him the truth. But I gave him the uncut version. It started affecting his schoolwork, and his grades started slipping. He was already getting over having anger problems because he couldn't help situations that were out of his control. He became distant and my baby boy wasn't saying much. All the lies and stories just wasn't adding up, I wanted everything in the world to believe my husband, but when you come home after 4 days and tell me a story about why you had to stay out and it sounds like some made up story out of a comedy book, what would you believe? I laugh at this story he told me every time I think about it. I will never know what was real or not, but it didn't add up at all. This man came home after being gone a few days, always leave on a Thursday night or Friday, which is payday at midnight for him.

Doing the week, we went grocery shopping and he was left with our food stamp card. I wasn't worried about the card because I didn't think he would spend any money off the card because he would be taking food out the kids' mouth. KMSL! I called the card just to be sure, because I really didn't trust him. The stamps were still there, but not the next day there was a nice amount missing off it. Now I'm thinking, why or what would he spend this on? In the past, I had to cancel bank cards just to keep him from spending the rest of the money. He got his pay check and the stamps. No way he was going to spend all that.

Another laugh in my face. Every time I try to give him the benefit of the doubt, I would be let down. At some point I had to realize that my husband wasn't going to change or do right, not even by his kids. When he eventually came home, it would be the first thing I would ask. He would try to avoid me, so he would keep watch on the house, wait until the lights go out and I go to bed, then he sneaks in the house and go sleep in another room. Sometimes he would wait until the next morning after I leave the house, and when I get back, he would be there. That day when we spoke, he told me that he was with some white friends and he didn't have cash to put up for his half of the cow.

Instead, he brought all the food they needed for the BBQ they were having while cutting up the cow, so he can get his half. That's where the stamps went. So ok, good investment I guess. We get a freezer full of meat in exchange, but one problem. Where is the cow? "Well you see, we was on the boat," he says, "and when I was getting off, my ice chest slipped into the water and when I was trying to catch it, it hit my foot hard and I let it go." So, you are telling me there are no stamps and no cow? Lol! I had to laugh to keep from crying. He asked, "why you think I'm limping?" Maybe because you just made this sh*t up and you expect me to believe it. He goes to the E.R. hopping on one foot and come back with the other foot wrapped. Even his brother said he saw him on the other foot when he first came in the yard. SMDH! How many lies this man has. Well, he had plenty. My husband was robbed so many times I lost count, and they all started to sound alike. You know there is always one to stand out over all. The funny thing that stands out about them all, it's always at an ATM on payday at 12 a.m. As he would put it, he was robbed by some young cats or he lost his wallet or his ID, or he forgot his ID, had to go back for it, then money would be gone. Sometimes you need a reality check, and if that was not my reality check...if that was not my wake-up call, I don't know what was.

CHAPTER 12

12

MENTAL BREAKDOWN

I do believe everything happens for a reason. My eyes definitely were not open. I saw only what I wanted to see, sat back and watched. I was too open to people, and I gave my heart and they tore it out of my chest. I just thought everyone was against me and laughing behind my back.

I was a mess inside. I felt like I was living a lie, and I was. I was lying to myself by convincing myself that change was going to come, but when? The only change that kept coming my way was us going downhill. Every day it was something new. With my husband it was a new lie, and at our home another bill going undone. We had got in so much debt, there wasn't a way out. I started having flash backs before all the drama started, before I became the person that I had become. I was a cold-hearted b*tch! I wanted to know how I got to that point.

I busted my a** after I got out my past situation. I worked hard, started banking money to the point of wanting nothing; and gambling, drugs, alcohol, and living a lie of a life consumed my husband. He was sick and needed help, but he was in denial and everyone was against him. I eventually broke down, tore up my house, and started screaming for dear life. Right then it all hit me and I thought I was at the lowest of the low that I could be. I was hurt. I fell to my knees and I cried out. I yelled, I screamed, I cried, I kicked, I broke things, and in the midst of it all, I snapped back. It's like a switch went off. I kept repeating, "No this is not you, this is not you who you are!" And, "It's not who you going to be, you're better than this and you can overcome, you can overcome anything you set your mind to." For all those who said that I can't and I won't, I said I can, and I will!

So, I got to thinking how I could take a negative situation and turn it into a positive situation. That's when I knew I had to turn my life over to God and ask for guidance, and say help me and give me the strength that I need to overcome. I didn't go to church much, but I knew God was real and could make a way out of no way. I see what He done for me. I could have been dead when I was hit by that drunk driver who left me laying in the ditch, when I thought about taking my life. When we somehow got food when we had nothing eat. When we had a roof over our heads because someone took us in when our lights were out. I know what He can do; He did it for me time after time again.

The choice was mine to sink as low as I could be and just give up on life, or to turn my life over to God because I know he could fight my battles for me. Still, I did nothing about it and continued to live in my darkness. It's a Saturday. I had returned home from paying a bill and my kids were all over. One by a nanny, one by a grandmother, and another playing with friends. I didn't know where my husband was. I knew he was around somewhere. I had company over at my house waiting on me. As I walked in to get settled, I see a stranger in the yard. A minute later, everything went out. My lights were disconnected. I be d*mn! I had just hustled the money for our water and gas bill. Banking on the paycheck the next week to pay at least a month's payments on our lights. I was so embarrassed! I called to see what needed to be paid for our lights, but what we owed, there was no way I could afford it. I had been getting by for a long time, but this time was different. I took my other child over to his grandmother and went back home to pack up some things for us before dark, and to fuss with my deadbeat husband. Over the next few weeks, all I did was cuss him out. He had come stay with us until I told him it was his fault and he had to leave. He would come over, and after sleeping all day, act as if everything was ok. That made me angry! For the past two years prior to us leaving our home, we had been separated in our home. I was in the master bedroom while he stayed in another room down the hall. I was sick of him and couldn't stand that man any longer.

He was still working and would give me a few dollars to put towards the light bill, while promising to do better and get his family back home. The next payday he was nowhere to be found. It was like he had fallen off the face of the earth. From that Friday until Monday morning, nothing. No call, nor nowhere to be found. Later that day, I would find him at his parent's house in his old room in bed sleep. He tells me he had been jumped by some guys and they took all his money. Didn't call the police or nothing. Now who he think is going to believe them pack of lies? Not me. He pushed me over the top. I politely closed the door and went back to my kids. The next day, he was like, "do you see my scars they gave me?" I said, "yes, I see, but why do they both look alike and got the same form and size?" As if he had done it to himself and i was fresh. If he was jumped on a Friday, it's 5 days later. It should have had some type of healing. This man thinks I'm a fool. couldn't even blame him no more. It was my fault for letting him continue to fool me, and he did a good d*mn job. Over the next few days I felt numb. I felt nothing. I wasn't happy nor was I sad. It was like I didn't even exist. I don't even remember getting up. I don't remember the day or the hour. The only thing I can remember is going to take a walk. I don't even remember where I went. I just knew I wanted to avoid certain people, but I ended up running into someone who worked my last nerves.

They were talking to me, but I wasn't paying them no mind whatsoever. All I was thinking about was no matter what I did, it wasn't right, or they found some fault at everything that person was the only one that felt that way. Everyone else thought I was doing an amazing job. As I try to avoid them, as much as I tried, I couldn't. Once I finished my conversation, we both went our separate ways. But somehow, I ended back on that same street, lost with a set of keys in my hand. I had found myself in front of the church, keys in hand. I opened the door. Once I got in, whatever state of mine I was in, I snapped. I locked the door and broke down and asked God to please help me take it all away. I give it all to you, Lord. I just need you right now. Shedding tears after tears, I know this life must be better than what I was experiencing. Just kept saying how sorry I was for all the things I did or didn't. Thanking Him because I didn't end up in no mental hospital or worse. I felt like I had it all, but I didn't. I felt like I was a hypocrite and I wasn't practicing what I was preaching. Telling my kids what not to do but living and allowing what I don't believe in to continue to happen. It was all my fault why I was made to be the crazy one. I poured my heart out to God at that moment. Afterwards I picked up my phone and called my pastor. He didn't answer so I left a voicemail asking him to please call me. I also sent a text.

My phone rang. It was a helper of mine looking for me and I told him where I was. When he came, he asked why I was there, and I told him I needed to be here. He asked if I was ok. After assuring him I was, he left and he went to my house. I was far from ok and lying in church. Who was I? I sat there and just talked with God. I wanted to walk in a new light. My phone rang again. This time it was the pastor. He said he had just got off the plane and the first thing he noticed was a text from me. When he checked his voicemail, he heard in my voice that something was wrong and he immediately called me. He said he wasn't going to be able to make it to the church to talk to me, but he was willing to stay on the phone as long as I needed. Once I explained to him what was going on, he said he would pray for me. We prayed together. After talking with the pastor and praying to God, I walked out the church and locked the doors. As I stepped outside, I was no longer scared. I felt like any fear I had was no longer. The sun was much brighter and everything much clearer. I don't know what happened, but the old me was no longer. It was the beginning of something new. I felt it in every part of me. What I did next didn't even worry me. I decided to leave for good. I went to the house and packed a few pieces of clothes for each of us, and walked out the door. No looking back. I left our home we worked so hard for. I left my husband I worked so hard to keep us together as a family. I left the lies, stories; everything that was not of God I left.

It was time. Although I had made up my mind to do what I needed for my kids, it was for me. I had to go find myself. I had to face facts and have that heart to heart talk with my husband. I told him that day I was leaving. I don't think he took me serious because I have left before and went back after he told me what I wanted to hear. Not this time. For 3 days I cried over the thought of it. All I wanted was my family, but were we better off in a broken home than us being whole? I was no longer in love with my husband. The love I had, it was gone. We lived in the same house down the hall for almost 2 years, fussing and fighting, no intimacy or any nothing. I had to explain that it wasn't right for any of us to keep putting our family through the bullsh*t. If it was meant for us to be together, we will find our way back someday. It was very hurtful to watch 20 plus years of our lives go down the drain. It was one of the hardest and hurtful things I had to do. I never experienced so much pain than I did on that week.

LIVING IN FEAR

Abuse can inflict physical and emotional wounds. Shame and fear can lead to isolation and lack of understanding. I am not proud of the things I did to cope with the things that happen, but I can't take them back. Part of growing up is realizing that people aren't always nice, and sometimes those you thought you knew so well will destroy you. To have people closest to us treat us worse than any stranger could, well, I feel my life as a child was stolen from me. My virginity was taken from me.

That is supposed to be a woman's most prized possession. I will never get that first time back to share with the one I love. To top it off, I was afraid to leave my husband after what he had put me through, afraid of another relationship in fear of sleeping with someone because he was the only man I was with for years after those situations. For years I had nightmares and flashbacks of the trauma that I had experienced from my childhood and adulthood. The memories of the abuse troubles me, and the pain, confusion of it all is painful. I have a lot of questions for them all. Some of them I don't even know, some I don't remember, one has passed away, and others I have confronted but are in denial. All I want to know is why. Why me? To my abusers, "Why me?" To my father "Why me?" To my ex brother-n-law, "Why me?" "WHY ME?" I suffered from anxiety and PTSD, and before I even knew what all of those was, I knew something was wrong with me. Every time I wanted to tell, I would get nervous about it. Even after I decided not to tell, I still would have this feeling in my body that I couldn't explain. I don't know if it was because I didn't tell or what. Sometimes my body would feel like something was crawling on me. Now I didn't start feeling like that until after the incident with the spider and I thought it was following me. I ran from one room to another, and so did the spider. I ran and jumped on top of the kitchen table and the spider ran up the wall behind the table.

I freaked out so bad, and the whole while my dad was having a field day laughing at me. I would always feel as if that spider attracts me and was crawling all over me. My body would get hot. I think about how I felt the day my daddy burnt me with a light bulb and scarred my back. Those things make you feel like you are reliving that all over again. It's a very sad thing to say you late someone, but for a long time I hated them all. Until this day I don't have much to say to my dad. I forgave him but I don't have nothing to say to him. Living in fear have you afraid to take risks and go for what you really want. You convince yourself that you're less than life. When you let fear run the show, you forget how to dream and are steady fighting that battle inside you that you feel no one would understand. When you are afraid you say yes when you really want to say no. Becoming a people pleaser, afraid of resentment. You say no to yourself when you should say yes, say yes to your dreams and goals, but you are afraid to fail. You become numb and your inner thoughts control you. You are always emotional. I just cried for no reason, and when somebody told a joke the whole room could be laughing, I wouldn't find it funny.

Numbness feels like I need a drink, because I can't, just want to stay in my night clothes and watch TV. That was me. For some people it's drugs or sex. I didn't do drugs because I was against it after what we went through behind my dad using drugs. As for as sex, well I could care less if I got it or not, even when I wanted it. Fear feels like no confidence in yourself, afraid to speak up when you need to. Fear sometimes made me controlling. I became hostile and ugly. You don't like the person you become, but you don't do anything about it. Fear causes inner and outer pain, sickness that comes in a form of fatigue, depression, sadness, hopelessness, anxiety and many others. You do things that would have a temporary relief that leads you back to square one or worse. Fear had me in the hospital thinking I was having a heart attack. I sometimes get hot flushes or chills or feeling like I can't breathe. Fear of being bullied, being hit, being touched; fear of just being. Living in fear would make you lock yourself inside and not come out, like the time the lawyer called me and said the guy that hit me broke out of jail and he might come looking for me. The time when a stranger was stalking me even during the day, afraid that I would be raped again. Just afraid of everything. I no longer want to live in fear!! I'm speaking out!!

I was reminded that there's no storm that God won't carry you through. No bridge that God won't help you cross. No battle that God won't help you win. No heartache that God won't help you let go of. He is so much bigger than anything you will face today. Leave everything in His hands and embrace this day confidently knowing that He will take care of you. Living in fear had me missing and it is time for me to find myself. This caterpillar is about to come out of her shell. I got to always remember that no matter what I go through or what life throws at me, my current situation is not my final destination.

RESOURCES

f you are going/went through something or you know someone that s going through something and need help whether It's abuse, gambling, bullying, etc..here are a few resources for you.

National Sexual Assault Telephone Hotline

Call 800.656.HOPE (4673) to be connected with a trained staff member from a sexual assault service provider in your area.

https://www.rainn.org/about-national-sexual-assault-telephone-hotline

The Childhelp National Child Abuse Hotline is staffed 24 hours a day, 7 days a week, with professional crisis counselors who have access to a database of 55,000 emergency, social service, and support resources. All calls are anonymous. Contact them at 1.800.4.A.CHILD (1.800.422.4453).

https://www.childwelfare.gov/topics/responding/reporting/how/

National Domestic Violence Hotline

+18007997233

https://www.thehotline.org/

Stop Bullying/ Bullying Prevention

https://www.stopbullying.gov/

https://www.pacer.org/bullying/

Substance Abuse and Mental Health Services Administration

https://www.samhsa.gov/find-help/national-helpline

Suicide Prevention

We can all help prevent suicide. The Lifeline provides 24/7, free and confidential support for people in distress, prevention and crisis resources for you or your loved ones, and best practices for professionals. 1-800-273-8255

https://suicidepreventionlifeline.org/

National Problem Gambling Helpline

1-800-522-4700

https://www.ncpgambling.org/help-treatment/national-helpline-1-800-522-4700/

Post-traumatic stress disorder

https://www.health.govt.nz/your-health/conditions-and-treatments/mental-health/post-traumatic-stress-disorder

Mental Health Treatment

1-855-834-2416

https://www.mentalhealthline.org/?n=8445494266

Made in the USA
Columbia, SC
26 September 2023

23241055R00098